Too Scared to Run
By Rossilyn Lillard

Too Scared to Run

Copyright © 2017 by Rossilyn Lillard

All rights reserved. No parts of this book may be reproduced or transmitted in any form or by any means without written permission of the author except in the case of critical articles or reviews.

Send all request to: writerrozzie@gmail.com

This is a work of fiction. The events and characters described here are imaginary and are not intended to refer to specific places or persons dead or alive. Any resemblances are purely coincidental.

Rossilyn Lillard

Acknowledgements

I would like to acknowledge God for allowing me to have the wonderful gift of writing. My children, Crystal, Stanley and Antwon whom I love and appreciate, have provided encouragement and motivation in helping me cross the finish line. They believed in me when I doubted myself. My children inspire me in many different ways. I see myself in each one of them. My thirst for knowledge and growth keep me reaching for what others may believe to be impossible.

A special acknowledgement goes out to Deidra Ds Green and the Mahogany Writer's Exchange. Editor, Chyta A. Curry of The Write Way and Angel Bearfield of Dynasty's Visionary Designs for their role in in getting this project launched. With their support my first novel is born.

It's not always about how you start but, how you finish. My dreams were reachable and I am living them today.

Follow me to get updates on events and new releases.

Facebook: http://www.facebook.com/ureadiwrite
Instagram: @ureadiwrite
Twitter: @Rozlillard

Dedication

This book is dedicated to my mother, the late Freddie Viola Lillard. She so wanted to read my first manuscript. She would have been proud of my accomplishment in seeing this to its completion and publication.

Always loved and forever missed.

About the Author

Rossilyn Lillard was given the gift of writing. She began writing short stories and poems as a young teen. This is her debut novel and soon to follow will be the sequel, Loss of Fear, Victim Turned Vigilante. She uses her creativity, life experiences and observances to create stories anyone would enjoy reading. Rossilyn is an avid reader who enjoys fiction. She has a passion for drama, contemporary women's fiction and Mystery. She received a Master's degree in Human Resource Management and Public Administration from National University in San Diego, California. When Rossilyn is not reading, she is writing and polishing up her craft. She currently resides in California where she enjoys spending relaxing times with her children, and grandchildren. She enjoys the simple pleasures in life. Outdoor concerts, plays, movies and making the best of the life given to her.

Chapter 1

The night we waited for all year was finally here, New Year's Eve. I waited all day for this night to arrive and it was finally here. I was feeling a little too tired to go anywhere. To be honest, I was feeling sorry for myself and all I wanted to do was go home, peel off my clothes, kick off my shoes and curl up with a good book with some nice music playing in the background. Anyway, I didn't even have an outfit picked out yet. I just couldn't believe another year had come and gone, without me meeting Mr. Right. I guess I'd better make my way home and pick out that outfit that will scream "Here I am, take me ."

On my way home, I stopped by my girl's apartment to tell her I changed my mind and decided I wasn't going. She looked at me and said "girl, are you crazy? This is the biggest night of the year, so snap out of it and get your ass ready for a great party." One of our closest friends threw the party to remember every year and this was to be the best one yet. Rumor had it that plenty of available men would be there. Lord knows I need to snag me one of them. As I walked back to my car she yelled, "Hurry up so you can pick me up by nine!" I yelled back, "Okay, okay already!"

As I drove down the Boulevard, I could feel the excitement in the air as men and women hurried about in anticipation to what the night would bring. Reaching my apartment, and pulling into my carport, I saw my neighbor, Mike. He shouted out to me, "hey, Arlene, I'm having a few friends over tonight. You know you're always welcome if you're not doing anything tonight!" I heard him mumble "when, do you ever do anything?" I shouted back, "I heard that." He yelled back, "Girl, you know I'm just playing." "Thanks, but I'm actually invited to a party tonight." Mike was my gay neighbor who lived next door with his boyfriend. A party to Mike was three or four other gay guys sitting around listening to oldies, drinking cheap wine and having sex all night. Curling up with a good book sounded much better, even if I wasn't going out. Now, don't get me wrong, Mike was cool and everything, but let's just say we have different taste when it came to having fun.

Turning the key in the lock and opening the door made me realize just how unexciting my life was right now. I pulled the blinds back to allow a little natural light to shine through the room. I stood there gazing out the huge, picture window wondering what was in store for me in the near future. I've always feared the worse; either dying tragically in a car accident or at the hands of some man. That thought always made the hair on my arms rise. Well, either way I would be dead, wouldn't I? Mike was right, when do I ever do anything, besides work? I snapped myself out of it long enough to tidy up my apartment before heading off to my walk-in closet to find that come catch me outfit for the party.

To set the mood, I put on "Got to Give It Up." It lifted my spirits enough to really want to get out the house for a change. It was already past seven o'clock and you know how long we girls take to primp, especially on New Year's Eve. So, on my way to the closet, I turned on the shower with the water as hot as I thought I could stand it. Maybe the tensions and stresses of the day would fade away if I stayed under the steaming water long enough.

If I must say so myself, I had really good taste in clothes. My closet could prove it. I didn't know what I was in the mood to wear, but I did know it would be a dress, a short one. I had plenty to choose from. If you walk into a party and want heads to turn, you have to show off your assets. My greatest asset had to be my big, sexy legs. What better way to strut those assets but in a short red or black dress? I picked out a red, strapless number with the built-in bra that made my girls look perky like the boobs women pay all that money for and still didn't look any better. I pulled out a pair of three-and-a-half-inch, black, satin strapped sandals. The sandals would accentuate my legs and the red polish on my toes would set it all off. I'm not much of a jewelry person, but for this occasion, I put on a pair of ruby-red and clear rhinestone earrings that dangled into the shape of a teardrop with a matching necklace and bracelet. Since I was going all out, I grabbed my black, satin pouch with the drawstring strap. It was big enough to hold my keys, money, ID, lip gloss and gum. In case I got lucky. I always carried a purse small enough for me to dance with so I wouldn't have to ask one of my girls to hold it for me. They would be on the dance floor before me. Tonight, we were party bound.

    The water running down my body felt so good. I lingered on the thought of what it felt like to have a man rub my body and give me the sensations water couldn't. I closed my eyes for a moment reminiscing back to when I had a man in my life. It felt good, satisfying and fulfilling. I dreamt of a time in my life when or if I would ever find love again with Mr. Right. I was wasting time because having a man in my life would only complicate things for me. I'm too involved with work to spend any quality time with a man. The fantasy inside my head was growing bigger and more unrealistic so I turned off the water. I felt revived and ready to take on the world when I stepped out the shower. I pat myself dry and rubbed lotion over my entire body, then I sprayed my favorite perfume. I sprayed on a little extra just in case I did meet Mr. Right. After getting dressed, I styled my hair into an upsweep with little curls on each side. I pinned it up with cute, little, rhinestone bobby pins. Let's not forget the baby hair. One last look in the mirror told me I looked hot and ready for the night and whatever came my way.

Heading north on the Boulevard, I noticed the night air was cool and the stars were shining brightly, illuminating the sky. It was going to be nice bringing in the New Year with my girls. I had a feeling this may be my lucky night. When I pulled up to my girl's apartment, I noticed a couple cars I didn't recognize in the driveway. I parked and got out to the sound of loud music. "Backstabbers" was playing on the stereo and boy did that bring back memories. I had lots of fun loving nights with the sound of them playing in the background, at parties, clubs and with men. Wow, what a life I thought I had back in the day.

I knocked on the door, but there was no answer. The music was so loud that whoever was inside couldn't hear me knocking, so I just let myself in. Standing in the living room was a nice-looking guy dressed in what we call church clothes. He turned around when he heard the door close and stared at me for what seemed an eternity. He finally found his voice and spoke. I spoke to him and thought, now this is a nice-looking man, I wonder who he is? My girls walked out the kitchen into the room where the two of us were; both with drinks in their hands. I shoved my girl on the shoulder and looked over to the man standing in the room. I wanted an introduction and couldn't wait to find out if he was single or not and why I never met him before.

His name was Demetrius. He was the brother to one of the most popular families in the neighborhood. I didn't know there was another brother that I had never met. He sure was fine and appeared to be nice and intelligent; unlike his thuggish ghetto ass brothers. I wonder why I never heard anyone mention this brother before. I've known his brothers and sisters for a long time. We even went to parties together. Everybody in the hood knew his family because of their gang and drug involvements. Trust me, they were no strangers to the law. Each one of them had been locked up at least once and for that reason alone, people feared them on the streets. I thought it was strange that Demetrius was never mentioned by anyone. Oh well, stranger things have happened I'm sure.

After the introductions, we talked about our plans for the evening. Demetrius was on his way to church for Watch Night. That explained why he was so sharp, all decked out in his black suit with white pinstripes, burgundy shirt and matching tie. He even had his bible with him. I was so impressed about him being a church man because nothing I did would get my ex-husband to church. Lord knows I tried. I went to church whenever the church doors were open; it was a habit from childhood. I told him about the party we were going to his and he told us we should be going to church. His response made the hair stand up on my arms and it gave me a good feeling inside. Being raised in church myself allowed me to appreciate the fact that this fine man was going to church instead of going to a sinful party on New Year's Eve. I bet those rowdy ass brothers of his weren't going to any church.

Rossilyn Lillard

It was getting late and the party awaited our arrival. When we were ready to walk out the door, I noticed Demetrius picking up something from the couch. It was shaped like a shotgun or rifle in a case. I asked him about it and he told me it was for bringing in the New Year. "You know, a couple shots in the air, that's all." I knew this to be tradition. My father still shot in the air at least once to ring in the New Year so I wasn't surprised to hear his answer. Demetrius and I said our goodbyes, but not before exchanging glances at each other. He asked if we were staying out all night because he would be out of church by 1:00AM and he could join us in partying the rest of the night. My girl, always playing the match maker, told him we would be back by that time or no later than 2:00AM. He left smiling because we agreed to keep the party going until he got back. He sure did look good and he was a church man, Lord, have mercy on me. Something told me Demetrius and I were making a connection in the house. That made the hairs stands up on my arms.

Wow, it felt good being out after all. My girl agreed to drive and that made it even better. We were driving down the Boulevard and traffic was a little heavier than usual due to all the clubs and house parties happening around town. Everybody and their mama was out wearing their best outfits and fancy hairdos; undoubtedly on their way to nearby clubs to bring in the New Year. I couldn't blame them though, it was a beautiful night. I knew the girls and I were about the best looking women out. We were fine. I knew we had to catch something. At least one of us should anyway.

Chapter 2

The party was jumping, Temptations played in the midst of all the party-goers trying to hold conversations. We stepped into the room and gasped at the beautiful decorations. Everyone was full of the New Year spirit, wearing party hats, blowing whistles and horns and wearing Mardi Gras masks, hiding their identity from their partners. Lots of stares from some of the women because they knew we looked better than they did. The three of us in unison said "don't hate." We laughed and kept walking, trying to find Beverly to let her know we had arrived and were ready to party. We found Beverly in the den talking to the DJ. She was yelling at him to play some cha-cha music. She wanted to dance but the cha-cha was the only dance she knew. As the DJ looked for some music to play, we talked and caught up on the events of the week. We gossiped about who was with whom and who shouldn't be. I told her she threw the best parties around and every year they just kept getting bigger and better.

"Girl, how can you afford it?" I asked not really expecting an answer

I asked Beverly if she knew about Demetrius. She said she never met him, but heard there was another brother. She also heard that he had been away for a while, but not sure where he was. She told me to stay away from that family because they were all bad news. I took that bit of information and tucked it away. However, I found this very troubling, but I let it pass. I didn't want any bad news or negative vibes ruining my night.

The DJ was playing 'That's The Way of The World" and the party was jumping. We all grabbed partners and went to the dance floor. We knew almost everyone there so that made it very comfortable to ask a guy to dance. There were a few single guys there and a few women we didn't know, other than that we all knew each other. One of my girls caught the eye of a guy standing next to the DJ. She walked over and introduced herself to him. They chatted for a while until a young woman walked up and tapped her on the shoulder and said, "excuse me, but do we know you?" She didn't dignify her with a response, she gave him a dirty look, rolled her big brown eyes and walked away. She rejoined our little clique. Knowing we all witnessed what happened, she started laughing. We joined in calling him all kinds of names.

We were having a ball on the dance floor, showing off our best steps. We danced with each other instead of the guys that were next to us. We danced, ate, drank and laughed the night away. There were plenty of snacks like chips, dip, egg rolls, cocktail wieners and everything a party was made of. I ate so much, I thought I would pop right out of my dress. Wow, I had so much fun. I guess you know there was plenty of liquor and beer. Beverly even splurged on the best champagne for the toast at the stroke of midnight. We danced the night away. I would have missed it being caught up in my own uneventful selfishness and loneliness.

The moment that everyone anticipated all year finally arrived. Right before the golden hour, we grabbed our glasses filled with the best champagne and yelled out the countdown, ten, nine, eight, seven, six, five, four, three, two, one, Happy New Year! Everyone blew their noise makers, threw confetti and tossed their hats in the air. There were hugs and kisses from everyone; even from those we didn't know. The party was so much fun. I'm glad I decided to get out. It always made me feel good to be out with my girls. This would be the year my life would change. I could feel it.

The night went on this way until around one thirty or two o'clock. When the party was about to end, the guys got bold enough to ask the girls out or ask for their telephone numbers. You know at every party or club when they play that last slow jam, everybody starts looking around for who they think they could get lucky with. A couple of horny guys came up trying to get with me, throwing out their weak lines, but I gave them the cold shoulder. In the back of my mind, I was interested in one man. His name was Demetrius.

The party was over and everyone said their goodbyes and well wishes for the New Year. All I could do was think about how I couldn't wait to get back to my girl's place so I could see him again. The drive back to my girl's apartment seemed extra-long. On a normal night out, I was always tired, however, tonight I had plenty of energy. The party had lots of good music and great people dancing and partying all night. I guess the adrenaline rush was still there.

When we pulled up in my girl's driveway, I noticed a car parked in front of her place. I crossed my fingers in hopes that Demetrius was waiting for us to arrive from the party. We got out the car and approached the door. He appeared out of nowhere still wearing his church clothes.

"Hey, ladies, ready to get your after party on?" The sound of his voice startled us and we let out little screeches.

"Where in the hell were you when we pulled up?"

"I was on the side of the apartment taking a leak," he said.

Was that creepy or what? Why didn't he do that before he left the church?

Once inside of the apartment, the party got started right away. My girl put music on and poured drinks. It just didn't seem right for Demetrius to be the only man at the party so we told him to ask a couple of his friends to come over and join us. When the guys arrived, they paired up with my two girls and it was on. Everyone was talking, dancing and laughing about what resolutions they made for the New Year while Demetrius and I sat on the couch talking and revealing information about ourselves to each other.

I didn't know where he was or why he was being kept a secret, but I was falling in love. He came off as caring, hardworking and loveable. He had the sexiest smile I've ever seen on a man. He was a sharp dresser. I liked that about him. He was very charming and attentive. When I spoke, he didn't interrupt like my ex did. Demetrius was Mr. Right, I just knew it. I believed the feeling was mutual. The Manhattans played in the background while we danced to one of their slow songs. It felt good to lay my head on his broad shoulders and feel his breath on my neck with his arm around my waist. It made me feel weak but safe at the same time. I closed my eyes so this moment would never end. When the song ended, Demetrius held me a little longer, caught me by surprise and kissed me full on the lips. I didn't respond at first because I didn't know this man from Adam, but I gave in and kissed back with a kiss so deep it left my head swimming. I only read about those types of kisses in books or in movies that I've watched. I didn't even know they really existed, that was up until this moment in time.

During my conversation with Demetrius, I didn't ask why I had never met him or where he's been. I wanted to keep things the way they were and not rock the boat. We danced and talked the night away until we both got hungry; likely from all of the drinking we were doing. My girls were caught up in conversations with the two guys that came over so Demetrius and I drove to the hamburger stand to get pastrami sandwiches. It was 4:30 in the morning. I was so hungry I couldn't wait to get back to my girl's apartment, so we ate in the parking lot. We were eating in one of the most dangerous intersections in the neighborhood. We must have lost our minds or did love cloud our senses. I knew the danger, but I felt safe with Demetrius. Eating in the car was such a big mistake because I dropped food all over my dress trying to eat the pastrami so fast. A piece of the pastrami fell on my dress. Demetrius picked it off and put it in his mouth real slow. If that wasn't a turn on then nothing was. My heart pounded wildly. I wanted him to ravage me right there in the parking lot of the hamburger stand, but I kept my composure because I knew the time would come and it would come real soon.

What has gotten into me, I didn't even know this man and I was already imagining the two of us in my king-sized bed making love in every way possible. I could see in his eyes that he felt as I did, but we both held back. We talked a little more and then drove back to my girl's apartment. When we made it inside, it seemed that the love bug hit. There wasn't a soul in sight, but we heard sounds coming from the bedrooms. We didn't want to disturb anyone so we sat on the couch and talked for a while longer.

When we saw the sun come up, we knew it was time to go. We exchanged numbers and promised to call each other later in the day. Driving off, I had the most wonderful feeling about Demetrius. He was warm and affectionate. That's something I longed for in a man. There were so many questions I should have asked, so many things I should have said, but it didn't seem to matter. A man that stayed out all night must be single, right? I mean, I stayed out all night and I'm single, so he must not be married. I pondered the thought as I drove down the Boulevard back to my place.

Chapter 3

During my conversation with Demetrius, I found out he lived fifteen minutes from me. That would make it convenient for us to visit each other. I liked the fact that he was as open about himself as I was about myself and that he appeared to be a down to earth brother. I must admit I had the strangest feeling that he was too good to be true. I tossed the thought aside and decided it was just the insecurity of not having dealt with a man for a while. I pulled into the car wash before it got too crowded to have them clean the inside of the car where I dropped pastrami over the seats and carpet. I could've done it myself, but my head hurt from drinking and I didn't want to make it worse.

After driving home from the car wash, I took a BC and waited about fifteen-minutes for it to take effect. I spent the rest of the morning cleaning my apartment. It had been a while since I gave it a thorough cleaning from top to bottom. I pulled the furniture away from the walls and vacuumed, cleaned the baseboards and dusted everything. I even removed the crystal from the china cabinet and cleaned it really good with ammonia; it was so clean that it sparkled behind the glass of the China cabinet. With the living room out the way, I headed toward the bedroom to tackle my closet. I have so many nice clothes, but I hate to give anything away. Name brand suits and dresses, designer jeans and shoes all filled the walk-in closet and now it was time to go through them and give some things to the Salvation Army. I started with the clothes on hangers first and then the folded jeans and sweaters on the shelves. Last to go were the shoes that ran the length of the closet. I admit that I'm obsessed with shoes. If they make them and they're cute, I'm buying them. After reorganizing the closet, I thought about my girls saying I had OCD because everything had to be in a certain order, you know, reds with reds, suits with suits, long skirts separated from short ones. You get the idea. It could be worse, I could be lazy or someone that never cleaned and have things all over the place.

Now that my apartment was clean and orderly, I stretched out on the couch to read a little. Over the past two weeks, I was so caught up in work that I didn't take time to read. It was time to play catch up with my favorite pastime. Nothing beats relaxing with a good book. Just as I opened the first page, the phone rang. It was Demetrius. We chatted for a few minutes and then he surprised me by asking if I was busy because he wanted to come by my apartment. Now,

I'm not the type of woman that gives out my address to strangers, but I felt comfortable with him so I agreed to let him come by.

The doorbell rang and I got up to let Demetrius in. He had on a pair of jeans and a long-sleeved shirt with a pair of basket weaved loafers. I was wearing a pair of sweats and a tank top. I fixed cold cut sandwiches and poured chips into a bowl before asking Demetrius if he wanted a drink. He felt like I did and only wanted a cold drink. I made a pitcher of lemonade and we sat on the couch eating lunch on TV trays. We were really making a connection and it felt natural talking to him. It felt like I knew him for years.

"Demetrius, tell me something about yourself."

"For starters, I'm an ordained minister. I preach every second Sunday at my father's church."

"I know the church. It's in my old neighborhood." I added.

"I admired my father from childhood. I wanted to follow in his footsteps and be active in the church. He left when I was a young boy, but I still kept in contact with him and continued to look to him for guidance."

"That's an incredible story, Demetrius. I've known your family for a long time. I don't recall any of them mentioning you before. No pun intended, but I'm shocked. Knowing the history of gangs in your family, I would not have guessed one of you was ordained."

We talked a little about his family, but he gave no indication he was connected to their illegal and unethical activities. What an amazing family. Gang members, drug dealers, dope addicts and who knew what else.

After a few hours of us hanging out, it was time for Demetrius to go. I still hadn't asked him if he was he married? We would be seeing each other tomorrow so I planned to pop the question then. We share some of the same interests and views on social matters and he was a student of the bible just like I was. We both could quote a verse of the bible at the drop of a hat and could tell you who wrote which books of the bible. We were impressed with each other's knowledge. This was drawing us closer even in this short period of time. I picked up my book to try and read a couple of pages, but my mind kept going back to Demetrius.

Chapter 4

It was time to prepare for work the next day, but I wished the weekend would have lasted a little longer. Like they say, "time flies when you're having fun." I laid out my clothes for the morning and washed my hair so I could start the week off fresh. I heated a frozen dinner, drank a glass of wine and called it a day. I couldn't sleep so I turned the television on scanned the channels to find a movie or something that would put me to sleep. After looking at the tube for a while, I got sleepy so I turned it off, fluffed my pillows and went to sleep.

Morning came before I knew it so I had to get up and start my week. I showered and dressed then went to the kitchen to make a bowl of cereal before leaving for work. I went to my carport, opened the car door, threw in my purse and got ready to get in the car when I looked around saw Demetrius standing at my car. I didn't see or hear him walk up. He almost frightened me when I turned around. Why was he sneaking around my place this time of morning?

"What are you doing here?" I asked.

"I just wanted to see you before you went to work," was his response.

"You almost scared me to death sneaking up on me like that."

"I'm sorry," he said leaning down to kiss me on the lips.

That dismissed any thoughts I may have had about him sneaking around. We kissed and said our goodbyes before I backed out of the carport and headed for work. What a sweet gesture, I thought.

As soon as I reached my desk, I called my girl to ask her if she ever experienced any problems with Demetrius and she told me that she hadn't. She told me to just enjoy the ride while it lasted. She asked what I was doing this weekend and reminded me that she was having a few people over for a barbecue and told me that I could bring Demetrius. She wasn't even curious as to why I asked the question. It could have been my imagination, but every time I mentioned him my girl changed the subject. I told her I allowed him to come over and visit, but I left out this morning's episode. I should just stop it because it had to be my paranoia kicking in.

I had piles and piles of papers on my desk that I needed to file and a number of calls to return, but I just kept thinking about him. Was he as sweet as he appeared to be or was this ploy just to get me in bed? Trying to remain focused was really difficult, but I managed to. I picked up the first message and started returning calls. After a few phone calls, I realized it was already lunch time. What would I eat? Where did the time go? I grabbed my purse, walked a few blocks to a little burger stand, looked at the menu on the wall and ordered fries, a burger with a Dr. Pepper.

As I ate my burger and fries, I people watched and wondered if anyone of them had as much on their minds as I did. I daydreamed of the future and tried to picture myself married with one or two children. It gave me a warm feeling inside. In the background was a large house with plenty of shade trees, white picket fence and a backyard for the kids to play in. The waitress brought over my bill and snapped me back to reality. I paid the bill and walked the few blocks back to the office.

I filed more from the stack of papers until they became little stacks of papers. I felt good with the progress I was making. I completed the reports that were past due on my desk. After a long day's work, I clocked out and headed off to the parking lot. Traffic was light for a Monday, especially for the freeway heading out of downtown. I thought this was due to New Year's weekend. After you party so hard on the weekend, it's hard to drag your butt out of bed to go to any job. I took the next off ramp so I could stop by the market to pick up a couple steaks to throw on the grill. I'm sure Demetrius would call and when he does I'll ask him over for dinner. I picked up a few other items and tossed them in the basket before checking out.

I got home, took the mail out the mailbox, opened the blinds and flopped on the couch to unwind. Even though I enjoyed my work, it still had me tired at the end of each day. It was nice to kick back, close my eyes and not worry about anything or anybody. The moment I closed my eyes the phone rang. I picked up the phone and Demetrius was on the line.

I didn't waste any time before asking, "have you made dinner plans?"

"I have not. I was calling to ask you out for dinner."

"That's nice, however, I wanted to prepare a home-cooked meal for you."

"In that case, I'll see you in an hour."

That gave me enough time to shower, get dressed and put the steaks on the grill. I made a green salad, baked potatoes and put a bottle of White Zinfandel and two crystal wine glasses in the freezer to chill.

The doorbell rang so I got up to let Demetrius in. He was wearing black slacks, white turtle neck pullover and black snakeskin shoes. He looked good. While he was standing outside the door, I quickly sized him up. He wasn't very tall, maybe 5'8" or 5'9" about 180lbs. Not a very big man at all, but he sure was handsome and he had a very charming smile. Needless to say, he knew how to dress and looked good in his clothes. If he was trying to make a good impression, he surpassed that the night I met him.

Demetrius thanked me for a nice dinner and dried the dishes as I washed them. We had a good time talking about the neighborhood and how it hadn't changed in years. I mentioned to him that I knew most of his brothers and sisters, but never heard anyone mention him. He thought it was because he was away, I thought it was strange all together. His sisters were cool, but I couldn't stand his sorry brothers. They rode around like the world should drop at their feet in fear and for women, they had their pick of any in the neighborhood. I told him I knew about his brothers' bad reputation on the streets and I sure hoped he didn't follow in their footsteps.

"Why have we not met before, Demetrius?"

"I was in prison."

He said it in such a matter of fact kind of way that I almost thought he said something else. To keep the conversation going, I asked him what he did. He ran down how he fell under the influence of drugs and alcohol while visiting some friends. He told me they were hanging out when he saw one of the neighbors walking to his car with a briefcase in his hand. He told me he ran up to him and asked for all his money. The neighbor froze in fear and dropped his briefcase. At that point, Demetrius reached for the briefcase, but the guy put up a struggle and that made Demetrius angry so he pulled a gun out of his waistband, pointed it at the man and told him to release the briefcase. The man continued to struggle with Demetrius when the gun went off causing the man to crumple to the ground. Demetrius grabbed the bag and ran like hell to get away before someone called the police.

He said he only ran about a block before the police sirens started wailing. He could hear the screeching of their tires behind him so Demetrius dropped the bag and threw his hands above his head as they approached. He was arrested and sentenced to a three to five year bid. He could've faced a harder sentence had the man died. He was released a couple of weeks prior to our meeting on New Year's Eve.

"I'm on parole for the next two years. If I don't walk the straight and narrow, I'll go back to prison to finish the rest of my sentence behind bars."

Wouldn't it just be my luck to meet a nice guy or what I thought to be a nice guy and he turned out to be a fresh prison parolee. My father always told me I knew how to pick them. Well, this time he was right. I picked a winner or had he picked me? His confession changed the mood of the evening. Demetrius must have sensed it and came over to me to explain. I was sick to my stomach and I felt light-headed. At first I pushed away, but he insisted that I listen to him and afterward if I still didn't feel comfortable with him around, he would leave and not see me or call again.

"Arlene, I've changed. I'm a different person than I was before. You see, I didn't know God the way I do now. I've repented from a sinful lifestyle, asking God to forgive me for all the wrong I've done."

"How can I believe you, Demetrius? Why should I believe you are any different than your brothers?

"They were a huge influence in my life before I went to prison. I've done some terrible things in my life. If I could do things over, I wouldn't repeat those same mistakes."

"What other secrets do you have, Demetrius? Are you married? Do you have children? What's your truth?"

"I am married, however, my wife and I have been legally separated for many years and we're waiting for our divorce to be finalized. No, I don't have any children."

With trembling lips, I asked him, "why should I take a chance on a man like you?"

He knew what to say and when to say it. "You told me you were a Christian, a believer in the most High. If you trust and believe God can change a man like me and turn my life around; then you should believe what I'm saying to you to be honest and true. God forgave me, can you forgive me and give me a chance, Arlene?"

He looked sincere and heartbroken. How could I judge him and turn from him at this point in his life? Demetrius needed someone in his life to be supportive and understanding. Because of the connection we made, I somehow knew I was that person. He needed a fresh start, a new beginning, a brand-new life.

There was an uncomfortable silence in the room that lasted what seemed like an eternity. Finally, Demetrius looked up at me and touched my cheek with his fingertips and stroked my face with the tips of his fingers. We looked into each other's eyes and stayed that way until he stood up and reached for my hand. He took me into his arms and held me close; so close that I could feel his heartbeat next to my own. I could feel his warmth, his need, his desire. I sensed that he could feel mine. He took me by my hand and led me to the next room; he then pulled me to the floor on top of him. I wanted him so badly that it hurt, but this didn't feel right. This was insane, I hardly knew this man and worst of all he was just out of prison. As hard as it was to move, I jumped up and asked Demetrius to leave. I needed some time to absorb the story I was told. I couldn't believe I almost made love to this stranger after he confessed to shooting and robbing someone. How could I have been so stupid, so weak and so blind?

I tossed and turned all night thinking about my conversation with Demetrius. I couldn't help but wonder why was this happening to me? What was the attraction that drew me to Demetrius? I had never met and connected the way I did with him. He was no better than his brothers. They were all from the streets and lived for the streets, why should I believe he gave his life to God? What made him stand out of the crowd? Was it his good looks, his charming smile or his gift of gab? Was I so desperate for a man that I would stoop to this or would I snap out of it and move on with my life? I've only known

Too Scared to Run

Demetrius for a few days and already he disrupted my life and invaded my thoughts. What kind of control would I allow this man to have over my life?

Chapter 5

The alarm went off and I hit the snooze button for a few extra winks before it was time to hit the shower. The pile of work on my desk should keep my mind occupied enough so I don't replay last night's events over and over in my head like a bad movie when I should have been sleeping. I hurried and get dressed so I could arrive at work a little earlier than usual. I would have enough time to get some work done while sipping my morning coffee. You know, sometimes you just want the world to yourself; well this was one of those moments. I wanted to escape the phony smiles and hellos to spend a little time with myself. Maybe then I could go about my day pretending everything was alright.

I went through the week attending meetings, creating presentations for upcoming meetings and brainstorming with co-workers on strategies for the next meeting. My mind was going out of control and it was a challenge to stay focused on what I was doing. Now, I have always been the type of person who could tackle any situation and come up with a reasonable solution. I knew this thing with Demetrius would work itself out and I would be back to normal in no time. I finished up with the day's agenda, turned off the light in my office and headed for the elevator.

On my way home, I stopped by the cleaners to pick up my dry cleaning. I thought about what I would cook for dinner. I passed a Chinese restaurant a couple of blocks back and decided to go back around the block and check it out. I looked at the menu for a moment and settled on the shrimp with chopped broccoli and fried rice. I headed home feeling exhausted due to the fact I didn't get much sleep last night. I ate and turned in early. I expected the telephone to ring, but it never did. I was happy about that. I dozed off eventually and fell into a deep sleep. Although the sleep was welcomed, I still couldn't rest easy. I felt uncomfortable, like I was being watched or something. I got out of bed to check the door and make sure all the windows were locked then I crawled back into bed and fell fast asleep.

The brightness of the sun in my bedroom made it impossible to sleep any longer. I get up, made breakfast and read the morning paper. Not much was happening in the paper so I showered and got dressed. A week or two passed since I visited the gym. I figured a good workout would stimulate my mind and allow me to think more clearly about the situation with Demetrius. The gym wasn't very crowded. I jumped on a treadmill and walked for about forty-five minutes before hitting the abdominal machines. After about ten minutes, I changed and lifted the weight bar for a few repetitions and then I called it quits and headed home.

Pulling into my carport, I saw my neighbor, Mike waving trying to get my attention. I walked over to him to see what he wanted.

"Arlene, guess what? There was a guy snooping around your apartment earlier today."

"What do you mean a guy was snooping around my apartment? What did the guy look like Mike?" I asked.

"He was approximately six-foot, medium-brown complexion and he was fine as hell. If he had stayed around any longer, I would have invited him to my place. Arlene, he was nicely dressed too," he added.

We both laughed knowing damned well Mike was not joking.

"He was looking through your windows on the side of your apartment. When he saw me, he left."

"Thank you, Mike." I said before going inside my apartment.

As soon as I got inside I pulled out my phone book and called Demetrius. When he answered, I immediately asked, "What were you doing snooping around my apartment?"

"I haven't been near your apartment, Arlene. I've been home all day."

"My neighbor saw a guy fitting your description, snooping around my door and windows today. Are you sure it wasn't you?"

"I would never snoop on you, Arlene. I have no reason to do anything like that. When I want to see you, I will call you or wait to be invited over. "

He stuck to his story that he was at home all morning and would never snoop around like that. I let it go and wondered who it could have been if it wasn't Demetrius.

Demetrius asked me if everything was alright, he told me I sounded strange on the phone. I let him know that I was alright and that maybe I wasn't getting enough rest at night and that could be making me a little edgy. We exchanged our little pleasantries and talked for a while about our previous conversation.

"I won't judge you for what you did in your past. I apologize for responding the way I did."

He sighed with relief and accepted my apology.

"We all make mistakes and should be forgiven by others especially after settling that debt behind bars." He said sounding remorseful. "If I hadn't given my life to God, I don't know where I would be."

I knew exactly where he would be. He would be on the streets, terrorizing the neighborhood just like his sorry ass brothers. I told him my girl was having a few friends over and he could meet me there if he liked. He in turn told me that she had already called and invited him and that he would be there. There she was, matchmaking again. Where would I be without my nosy friend? Well, one thing for sure, she always had my back when I was pressed against a wall.

Chapter 6

There were more people at the gathering than I expected. Demetrius had a couple of his buddies with him. The pit was blazing and there was enough liquor to start a small liquor store. Demetrius saw me and came over to greet me with a big smile and relief on his face. He gave me a bear hug and a kiss on the cheek. He was very charming and irresistible. His actions raised a few eyebrows from onlookers that wondered what was going on. Well they would just have to wait to find out because I wasn't saying a word. I would never count my chickens before they hatched.

Once again, Demetrius was attentive and occupied all my time to the point where I couldn't talk to any one person any longer than a minute or two before he would come over and steal me away from them. I was being swept right off my feet by this man and this had never happened to me before. This was nice. I felt like a princess spending the day with Prince Charming or something. If I moved away from him, for any reason, he would ask if I needed anything, water, drink or food. If I did need something, he would jump right up and get it for me.

"Would you get me another glass of wine please?"

Rossilyn Lillard

"Arlene, I think you've already had enough to drink."

I was a little disturbed by his response. I am a grown and very independent woman. I didn't need a man to tell me when I had enough to drink. I just smiled and thought to myself I know this man. This stranger is not trying to control me already. Hell, we have not even gone out on a real date yet. This is behavior that your man, your one and only would display, not some man you barely knew.

The day finally ended and I was preparing to leave when Demetrius saw me in the kitchen talking to my girl and asked to speak with me before I left. He wanted to know if I felt like going to his place after the party. I gladly accepted the opportunity to see how the other half lived. I told him I would follow him there if he was leaving. He quickly said his farewells and jumped in his car. I wasn't surprised to find he was driving a Cadillac. It was red with cream, leather seats and white wall tires. It was pretty but flashy. Just like its owner.

I jumped in my car and followed Demetrius to his place. It was a one bedroom duplex in the heart of gang territory. Better him than me because I would be too afraid to close my eyes at night. The thought of walking on the streets made be quiver inside. I quickly followed him inside. It wasn't what I expected for a flashy dresser like him. I thought I would see expensive furnishings, fancy rugs and décor but it was very simple. One thing that did catch my eye was the stereo system and entertainment center. It outshined the rest of the place, in fact it was very out of place. I spent the first few minutes looking for any signs of a woman but I came up empty. To make sure, I asked to use the bathroom because if there was a woman living there it would be certain personal items in there. Well, it was clean as a whistle, not even a hair anywhere.

Now, I could relax and enjoy the rest of my night. I was almost positive that this would be the night Demetrius would try to finish what he started a few nights ago at my place. I returned to where he sat on the couch and sat down beside him. He had Teddy Pendergrass, my favorite male artist playing on the stereo. I knew I was right about his intentions of inviting me over. Everyone knows Teddy was one of the sexiest, singing male vocalists out there and it's a fact that his music got many men and women in trouble. If Teddy was the last song of the night playing at a party or club, even the ugliest of men could get lucky and score. His music carried you away and when it's all over you're only left with regret.

Demetrius talked about how his marriage had failed and how he just wanted to move on and make a better life for himself. We talked freely about church, marriage and relationships.

"I grew up in a home with my father being the only one working and when it got to be too much for him, he walked out."

"How young were you when your father left, Demetrius?" I asked.

"I was in elementary school, fourth or fifth grade."

"That must have been hard on you and harder on your mother."

"It was a difficult time for my brothers and me. We didn't have that father figure in our crucial teenage years, so we took to the streets for guidance."

"When I got married, I promised God that I was marrying for life. I never planned on divorcing. I don't blame my wife for leaving me though. She was tired of the life I was living. I spent most of my time in the streets and it hurt our relationship. What about you, Arlene, what was the reason for your divorce?"

"My husband was verbally abusive from the beginning of our marriage. I didn't measure up to his standards as a wife. I was weak and I allowed him to belittle me to the point I believed I was nothing and deserved nothing. One day he hit me, blacked my eye. I pressed charges against him. I moved out while he was in jail. Six months later we were divorced. Two years out my life wasted."

"I would never hurt you, Arlene. Any man who abuses a woman is a coward. A woman should be loved and treated gently. I want to give you everything he didn't."

Demetrius told me he learned from his mistakes and was ready for a relationship.

"I'm not ready to make a decision as important as this. Let's take it slow and allow nature to take its course."

Demetrius agreed. "So what church do you attend?"

"I attend a small Church of God In Christ, never missing a Sunday."

"You should visit us one Sunday. We have a great sounding choir. The preaching is not that bad either."

"I'll do that," he responded. "I'm preaching this Sunday's sermon at my church. You should come."

I was interested in hearing him preach. "What time does the service start?"

"Service starts at eight o'clock in the morning. I hope you'll be able to attend the service."

The subject must have changed the direction of the evening because Demetrius didn't try anything, not even a kiss. All I got was a gentle hug when I got in my car to leave. He gave me directions to his church, said goodnight and I drove off. He was very clever to allow me to go to his place, listen to nice music but not try anything. It was like he could read my thoughts or something. He knew what I expected from him and he went the opposite direction just to fool me. Clever he was, but how long could he play the game. Furthermore, which one of us would win?

The next morning, I get out of bed, made myself breakfast, showered and prepared for church. The telephone rang. I wasn't surprised to hear Demetrius on the other end. He was checking to see if I was still coming to hear him preach. After I promised to be there, he hung up. I looked in the closet to find a nice, conservative outfit to wear. I didn't want to look like a tramp going to church service so I picked out a nice navy print suit and a pair of navy pumps. I put on a pair of small gold studs, sprayed my favorite perfume, grabbed a navy clutch bag and headed for the door.

Too Scared to Run

The church was a nice size and appeared to be well kept. It had a large parking lot next to it which made it easy for me to find a spot to park. I was a little early because Sunday school had not let out yet so I took this time to say a prayer for Demetrius in support of his sermon. I also prayed for the strength to resist temptation and weakness when it came to him. I didn't want him to have any control over me in any way. I wanted to go at my own pace and only when I felt the time was right, would I give in to his advances. What I needed to do was pray for the strength to avoid Demetrius altogether because in the back of my mind I knew something was wrong, but again I dismissed the thought.

As I walked inside the doors of the church, I noticed how beautiful it was; high beamed ceilings, tempered stained glass windows and a baptizing pool that sat behind the pulpit surrounded by three walls that were painted with angels and cherubs. It was such a serene atmosphere that gave me a peaceful feeling. I knew today would be a great day. I found a seat near the middle and sat down. I looked around the church. Everyone seemed to be caught up in conversations and busying themselves finding seats. I looked toward the back of the church and saw two of Demetrius' sisters and one of his brothers. They noticed me and waved hello. I was hoping they wouldn't sit near me. I got my wish when they all sat on the other side near the back of the church.

Devotion started and everyone took their seats. The pastor of the church cited the Lord's Prayer while the members read along silently. Afterwards, the choir marched in and did a musical selection. The choir was quite large consisting of both men and women, old and young. Their choir robes were very nice, emerald green with cream collars. They sang beautifully as they marched into the stands. They even had an organ and piano player and there was a drummer that looked to be no older than twelve or thirteen years of age. He must have had good training because he banged those drums exactly to the key of the music. As the choir sang their selection, I saw Demetrius and another man enter the pulpit and sit down in their respective places. I saw him scanning the room looking for me. Once he spotted me, he smiled.

The Deacon stood and asked all visitors to stand, state their name and the name of the person that invited them. Of course, I hated that part of visiting other churches. I stood when it was my turn and stated my name and that Demetrius Weaver invited me to hear his sermon. We were given a warm welcome from the church and then we took our seats. The choir sang another selection and then testimony service began. One by one the members of the church stood and gave their testimonies. Some of them cried as they spoke and others sang a few verses of their favorite song. After listening to some of their testimonies, I felt blessed to walk in my own shoes.

It was time for the sermon which was to be delivered by the one and only Demetrius Weaver, or Mr. Right as I called him. Demetrius stepped to the mic and asked everyone to stand while he delivered a prayer over the service. He asked the Lord to bless the readers and hearers of his word, in Jesus' name and then said, "Amen." He asked us all to open our bibles and turn to the book of Romans, chapters 14-15 and he began preaching his sermon. He preached on the weak and strong and how we shouldn't judge others.

I started to feel like Demetrius was directing his sermon to me. Was this a sermon that he selected prior to today, or did he jump into this after his encounters with me? He went on and on about the strong helping those that were weaker vessels and how we all belong to God in life and in death.

He mentioned the verse where one day we will all stand before God's judgment, so stop judging each other, stop placing stumbling blocks in the path of those we love, show kindness and peace, show understanding and most of all show forgiveness. I believe Demetrius was pleading for me not to allow his past mistakes get in the way of us. He told the church to allow those that are not sure to lean on our shoulders and be held up, do well and reap a good reward. "We have all sinned and fallen short of the goodness of God. God loves us all equally and only He can past judgment." He said.

Demetrius kept up his pace until the church got all in to it and started shouting, "amen, thank you Jesus and praise the Lord." You know how they do it in the black church, the man at the piano will hit a few keys which in turn are followed by the organist and drummer. That fed Demetrius' fire and he bellowed out the rest of his sermon in a deeper, stronger tone of voice that really sounded convincing and touching. Before I knew it, the church was standing on their feet, shouting and speaking in tongues. Demetrius delivered his sermon a confidence that I believe surprised even him. He reached his audience and touched something in them that made a connection. He looked pleased, his pastor smiled and looked pleased too.

In closing the choir softly sang "Give Your Life to Jesus" while Demetrius opened the doors of the church inviting all sinners and backsliders to come to the altar and give their lives to Jesus while they still had a chance. He asked them to open their hearts and allow Jesus to come in, while the blood was still running warm in their veins. I looked down the aisles of the church where men, women and children walked to the front of the church where the Deacons received them and the pastor prayed for them and anointed their heads with oil. The pastor introduced the newcomers to the church and they received the right hand of fellowship. The choir stood and did their final selection for the day, Demetrius said the closing prayer and church let out.

What a wonderful and surprising service. Demetrius was debonair and smooth, even in the pulpit. This man had a way with wooing people, whether it was romantic or interpersonal. He made everyone he came in contact with feel important and he always gave his full attention. I couldn't believe he preached his first sermon without stuttering or displaying any signs of nervousness. His religious convictions must be strong because only someone that truly gave their life to God and accepted Jesus as their personal savior would be able to stir up a church like he did. The spirit had to be upon Demetrius up in that pulpit.

Demetrius caught up with me in the parking lot before I reached my car. I told him how much I enjoyed his sermon and how the spirit moved in the church. He smiled at me as usual and thanked me for the compliment. He asked if I had plans for dinner later. I didn't so we agreed to meet at a restaurant in the Marina. I needed to stop by my apartment and change out of my church clothes for something a little more casual and relaxed. I checked my messages when I walked in the apartment and there were a couple of calls from my girls asking where I was hiding. They felt slighted that I was spending all of my time with Demetrius. I'll get back with them later, but right now, I had a man to meet for dinner. I changed into a white, lightweight sweater and a pair of black jeans. On my way out the door, I slipped into a pair of zebra print flats and headed to the car to meet Demetrius.

Chapter 7

It took about forty-five minutes to drive to the Marina and park. I walked in the restaurant and Demetrius was already seated at the bar. He walked over to greet me. We exchanged hugs and walked to the bar where he had a glass of wine waiting for me. He was having a glass of wine as well and chasing that with a shot of brandy. It must be nerves from that sensational sermon earlier. We sat at the bar for a while and then moved to the restaurant when our table was ready. Walking beside Demetrius gave me a visual of how he carried himself. He had a strong and confident demeanor. It felt good to walk next to him. He was wearing a casual jacket, brown corduroy pants and a white sweater and topped it off with a pair of brown and beige gator, lace up shoes. I would never need to worry about being embarrassed while I was out with him because he had that area of his life covered and I liked it.

Demetrius and I made small talk while we looked over our menu. I was famished so I ordered the T-bone steak and baked potato entree with a side of steamed vegetables and a piece of cornbread. He on the other hand ordered grilled catfish, garlic potatoes with a small dinner salad. He also asked the waiter to refresh our wine glasses. One glass of wine is usually all I can handle, but t I thought it was in order that I celebrate with Demetrius. It was of course a celebration; his first sermon and I was there to witness it. While waiting for our dinner to be served, we were really quiet. It was strange because he always had something to say. I was surprised to find myself at a loss for words.

"Why did you select that particular sermon?" I asked.

"I prepared a different sermon, but as I sat in the pulpit, the Holy Spirit changed the direction of what I would preach on."

He spoke as if he had no control over the sermon that was given to him. Either Demetrius was a great liar or the Holy Spirit really placed that sermon in his mouth this morning. I was having a lot of mixed emotions about that, but decided to let it go. If Demetrius was playing with God, he would get his just punishment. I wasn't the one to make that judgment call. After all wasn't the sermon about forgiveness and being non-judgmental toward others? I was really moved. This was drawing me right into this mans' arms, just where I wanted to be.

Demetrius told me he took his preaching style from his father and other ministers he heard preach in his younger days. He had an old soul; you know, the kind that appears older than they really are. He used that old soul wisdom to bring that church to their feet and rejoice the Lord. Maybe I was feeling guilty about Demetrius or even sorry for him for what he went through in his life. I expressed the good feeling I got when he was around. I said the unimaginable.

"Despite my earlier hesitation, I do want to be in a relationship with you."

He smiled. I was winning his heart and breaking through barriers of my own feelings. The uneasiness subsided.

"I was afraid to ask you about being a couple. I was afraid to mention having a relationship due to my past."

"I know how to forgive. I too have made mistakes. So Demetrius, does this make us an official couple?" I asked.

He leaned across the table and kissed me gently on the lips. I never wanted it to end. I wondered what was on his mind at that moment.

We ate our food and finished our drinks in silence. After dinner, we talked a little longer and decided to leave and drive back to Demetrius' place to have another drink and talk. I drove my own car but I took the scenic route because I needed to be sure I had a clear head when I arrived at his place. That way I wouldn't allow myself to get into a sticky situation without wanting to. I was sure Demetrius wouldn't wait for long before he took this to the next level.

Driving through the Westside always made me appreciate where I was from. The trees, the green grass and the snooty people made me appreciate the hood. It wasn't much, but it was home and everyone felt at home being there. We knew who to watch our backs from and it wasn't each other all the time. We had the same crime in our neighborhoods that everyone read about in the papers or saw on the news. Well they had crime over here too. It just wasn't showcased and advertised like it was over in the hood. They tried to keep theirs quiet, but it was there and getting worse all the time.

Demetrius must have driven like hell to get home so fast. When I knocked on the door he answered wearing nothing but his pants. Stepping in, he reached down and took off each one of my shoes so I could make myself comfortable. I walked over to the couch to sit but before I could, he grabbed me into his arms, squeezed me tightly, and started kissing me all over my body; from my lips to my ankles sending chills and shockwaves all through my body. He eased me down to the couch and slowly removed my top, my bra and my jeans. Stopping at my bikini, he untied the little strings on the sides of my panties one by one with his teeth. He gently eased my panties away from my yearning, pulsating body. I was afraid of what he was doing to me, but at the same time I wanted him so badly. I wanted to shout out loud "take me now!" My heavy panting must have caught his attention because he raised his hand to my face and touched my lips with his fingers while gently stroking my cheeks. He whispered ever so softly to me that he wanted to make love to me and that he would make my night special. I wanted to speak out, I wanted to scream for him to stop, but the words wouldn't leave my lips. As he kissed and stroked my entire body, I gave in to his control. This man claimed to be a man of God, how could he be doing this to me right now? Why was he taking advantage of me? Why was I allowing this to continue? He took me manfully into his arms. Unashamed of his need, he slowly thrust his manhood inside my body. I felt weak and vulnerable beneath him. I wrapped my legs around his small, muscular body. I started to silently cry as I unselfishly gave myself to him.

We lay quietly wrapped in each other's arms. It was so quiet, we could hear each other's heartbeat. I touched his body as hot sweat ran down his chest and body. I gently stroked his chest and forearms working my way down to his manhood. His body came alive with an urgency twice as strong as before and he took me again leaving all parts of my body wanting him even more. I was in ecstasy as our bodies entwined in a heated passion that I had never experienced before. I climaxed with this man like with no other man in my life before. I was in heaven. I knew for sure this was Mr. Right.

After our lovemaking session, I lay awake trapped with my own thoughts and feelings. I felt so guilty for allowing this man, this minister, this man of God to take my body. We committed fornication. It was wrong for many reasons. I knew it would eventually happen, but I did nothing to avoid it. I encouraged it and now I feel ashamed. I barely knew him; now what would he think of me? This man was a prison parolee, still married although separated and he committed a sinful act with me. For God's sake, what was I doing, what were we doing? My head was spinning so fast I couldn't catch up with my thoughts. I had to get up and get out of there without waking Demetrius. I could never face him after this. What kind of woman would he think I was? What kind of man of God was he? All of these thoughts invaded my mind as I got myself together to go to my own house.

Trying not to stir Demetrius from his deep sleep, I got off the couch and tiptoed into the bathroom to put my clothes on. I brushed my hair back and turned to leave. There stood Demetrius in the bathroom doorway. This man was like a cat. I didn't hear him make a sound. That's just a little creepy to me. He startled me and I jumped. He looked into my eyes. I knew he could sense the confusion I was feeling. He put his arms around me and I allowed my body to rest freely in his arms. He led me back to the couch and we laid there together. I forgot all about the guilt and shame from earlier. I laid there to enjoy the remainder of my special night. I forgot how good it felt to lay in a man's arms after making love. I felt safe and loved. I didn't want this feeling to ever leave.

Demetrius was such a gentle person. He took his time to please me in every way possible. This wasn't typical of most men. After they got theirs, you were on your own if you didn't get yours. His touch had meaning and it was talking to me. My skin felt alive when he touched it, he made the blood pump strong through my veins. I was in love with this man and I didn't know if that was a good thing or not. Looking into his eyes made me feel warm all over. I just wanted to remain in his arms forever. We didn't talk much after the lovemaking because the act spoke for itself.

It was getting later and later and I did need to go. This time when I got up, Demetrius put my shoes on each foot and kissed me long and hard at the door. He walked me to my car gave me a hug and told me to drive safely. I pulled off and as far as I could see in the rear-view mirror, he was standing on the curb watching until I got out of sight. My heart was still pumping with excitement from the night's events. I was in love with Demetrius and needed to know if he felt the same. I didn't want to appear childish and ask him. I waited to see how things would play out.

When I got home I called Demetrius to let him know that I made it home safely. He told me to get some rest and that he would talk to me in the morning. Before hanging up he said "Arlene, I love you." I was so shocked and excited at his words that I couldn't say it back quick enough. Finally, the words I love you come out and we said goodnight. I was the happiest woman in the world and there was nothing that could take that feeling away, absolutely nothing. Did love at first sight really exist or was it just a fantasy?

Too Scared to Run

Chapter 8

Monday morning came and I wasn't mentally or physically prepared to make it through the day. Not after the night I had with Demetrius. I wanted to lie in bed and rethink the night before, but I knew that was an impossible thought. It was still early, but I wanted to call my girl to see what she would think about Demetrius and I being a couple. I called my girl to get her input. She wasn't surprised to hear me say that I slept with him. She said to me, "enjoy him and stop worrying about it." I expressed my concerns about him fornicating, she only responded by stating that he was a man of flesh and blood just like the rest of us. Once again, she shrugged the subject off and started asking about me and my work. That little voice in the back of my head was trying to tell me something, I refused to listen to it.

I busied myself working hard at my job and at home to avoid thinking about what I did with Demetrius. Demetrius was consuming me and it felt both good and bad at the same time. I wanted a man and I got one. He was a good-looking godly man at that. He was such a charming man that I found him to be almost irresistible at times. I couldn't shake that feeling of something not being quite right about him. Could this be real or would I wake up one day and regret allowing Demetrius into my life?

We spent all our time together. We loved our families so we shared our time with them as much as we could. Everyone appeared to be happy that he found someone to love. They accepted me into the family and my family liked him a lot as well. He spent a lot of time at my place so we decided that we could save money by giving up one of our apartments. We decided to give up his place because he had too many memories of his ex-wife being there. He moved in, got settled and we lived happily together. He cooked, cleaned, made love to me and kept me as happy as possible. The perfect man any woman would want.

Week by week came and went until those weeks turned into months and those into years. For the last few months, Demetrius spent a lot of time away from home. I chalked it up to him being involved with the church. Whenever he would leave at night, he was always dressed as if he was going to church so I didn't question it. He got away with it because we still attended separate churches. We thought it would be best to keep our personal lives and living arrangements to ourselves because the church wouldn't condone one of their pastors fornicating and sinning the way we were carrying on. I did not like the dishonesty, but my love for him surpassed that guilty feeling. What we won't do for love. That old eerie feeling began to creep its way back into my life again. What was he doing?

After two years, Demetrius and I continued to be happy together. I had a feeling he was hiding something from me. I didn't know what it was. I knew it would come to pass sooner than later. I spent so much of my time with him that I barely spent time with my girls anymore. After a while, they stopped inviting me out with them. I didn't care because I had my man and was content. That is until lately.

I allowed myself to fall into a routine with Demetrius. I would go to work and back home day in and day out and it was starting to wear on me. When I got home, he would oftentimes be gone already, leaving me just a short note that he loved me and would be back soon. One evening after arriving home the phone rang and it was a collect call from Demetrius. He was in jail and wanted me to go to his brother to get money to bail him out. Being the blinded lover I was, I didn't ask any questions, I just did as he instructed me to. His brother gave me the money and the two of us went to pick him up from the jail. He came out, got into the car and we rode back to the apartment in total silence. When we arrived, he told me to go inside so he could speak with his brother for a minute. I went inside and waited for him to come in. Something wasn't right with this picture. I could feel it, something was way off.

Demetrius tried to convince me that it was just a simple mistake and that everything was okay. He would go to his court date and straighten everything out. Well, he had his court date alright. He was found guilty of violating his parole with possession of cocaine with the intent to sell. This had to be a mistake, Demetrius was a changed man was now a minister for God. How could this be happening to him? He was sentenced to one year in the county jail. This all happened so fast. I was in shock at the fact, my man was gone to do a year in a county jail. Did he revert back to his old ways or was this just a terrible dream?

I walked slowly out of the courtroom without looking back at him. I tried to grab on to the reality of Demetrius dealing drugs right up under my nose and I didn't know it. I felt like such a fool such, an idiot that was just played by the man she loved. I felt betrayed by him and everyone that knew him. Did my own friends, my girls know he was doing this and didn't tell me? I felt I could trust no one, not even them. It was hard to accept that my life, my safety was jeopardized by a man that so easily swept me off my feet. He was as much of a conniving snake as the serpent was in the Garden of Eden.

My Mr. Right was not the man he claimed to be. All the while he was pouring his heart out to me, he had been lying. He was just like his brothers; no good and still out in the streets. Was he out on the streets while pretending to do God's will? This was blasphemy, wasn't it? It was hard to do, but I had to face that fact that he was probably lying about the way he felt about me too.

I poured myself into my work, assisting clients, returning calls, following leads to stay busy and keep my mind focused on what was important and real in my life. I felt so depressed about the situation that all I did was sit by the telephone waiting for his call. Every day I waited and still no call from him. I guess he was too ashamed of himself to talk to me. Especially after telling me he changed. He owed me an explanation about the double life he was living. He owed me the truth. I tried to get information from his no-good brother, but he was certainly not talking. You know what they say, "blood is thicker than water." Hell, for all I know, it could have been him that was selling drugs and not Demetrius. Everybody always said they looked alike. I wanted answers.

I broke down and stopped by my girls' house. She heard Demetrius was picked up by the police, but claimed she didn't know the entire story or its outcome. As calmly as I could, I told her what I knew.

"I feel so stupid and used throughout this entire ordeal." All I could do was shout and yell at her for keeping this from me. "I thought we were girls that had each other's back. Now all I can think of is your betrayal. This was serious and you should have warned me to stay away from him, but you didn't."

For the first time, she didn't change the subject on me. By the time I left her place, I learned so much more about Demetrius than I ever could have imagined. He was a career criminal that was arrested for robbery, possession of firearms, possession of narcotics and domestic abuse. He spent more than half of his life behind bars, beginning as a juvenile. When I met him, he was just released from prison. I thought to myself, anyone can make a mistake, but what he's done is far more serious than I can deal with. His family, especially the brothers were known for being in and out of jail and he was no different than they were. Worse than that, he was pretending to be a man of God and that made him scary to me. Any man that can lie about God will do just about anything. Did his pastor know his past and if so how could he allow this pretentious man to stand in front of a congregation and talk about God and saving souls?

Chapter 9

While driving to my apartment, I thought back to the beginning when Demetrius and I first met. It was a great time in my life. He was a charming person that I believed in and had faith in, but it was all a figment of my imagination. He is one of the worse men that I have ever known and he moved into my life and home. I had to think of a way to get myself out of this. In order to do that, I needed to talk with Demetrius to see where his head was at. I wanted to hear from him so I could decide what I needed to do. I was not proclaiming to be perfect nor was I passing judgment, but this was just out of the question.

Two months went by without a word from Demetrius and by that time I had let go of some of the hurt and anger. I think it was all a part of his plan. He could see straight through me and figure me out so easily while at the same time fooling me into believing he changed. The telephone rang while I was in the shower. I jumped out and answered it only to find it was a collect call. I accepted and from the other end came his voice. Hearing his voice made me shutter. I could barely get out a hello before he started telling me how sorry he was and how he missed and loved me. I couldn't get a word in edgewise without him pleading with me to give him a chance and how all of this was a terrible mistake. I can't lie, it felt so good to hear his voice that all the negative vibes that I was feeling faded. All I wanted was for him to hurry and come home. I knew in my heart that if he could come home, he would make everything alright. He had to hang up, but would call me the next time he got the chance.

I had so many mixed emotions that I couldn't think straight. When this terrible nightmare first began, all I wanted was this man out of my life, but now I wanted him back home. Demetrius called me as often as he was allowed and that made the time away from him a little more bearable. We loved and needed each other. We didn't need to be apart any longer than we were already. Demetrius was down to five weeks, what they called short time. All he needed to do was stay out of trouble during these last weeks and he would be home free.

The weeks passed by quickly. It was finally time for Demetrius to come home. He wanted to take the bus home and asked me not to pick him up, so he could clear his head. I agreed and stayed home to tidy up and get my own head straight. I still had a lot of unanswered questions that only Demetrius could answer. I wanted to be prepared to ask them as soon as he got settled in. I wondered about his relationship with God due to known facts of men and women that claim to find God while locked up and then returning to their life of crime as soon as they hit freedom. Demetrius was so convincing about his new relationship with the Lord that I couldn't imagine he made it all up. I thought back to the Sunday he preached at his church; the sermon was so moving, could that all have been an act? I believe in him and pray that I'm not wrong about him. Deep down inside, I knew this was only the beginning of the hell he was going to put me through if I was wrong about him. Would I allow my selfishness to get in the way of the bare truth? Did I really find Mr. Right, or did I make the biggest mistake of my life?

Chapter 10

I prepared a nice dinner for Demetrius knowing that after a year of eating jailhouse food he would be ready for a real home cooked meal. I made his favorite, rump roast with red potatoes and green beans. I topped it off with a hot pan of cornbread. He should be famished after the long bus ride home. I took a shower and put on a sexy lounger to welcome him home in. I dabbed on a bit of his favorite perfume. I was sitting on the couch when I heard his key turn in the lock. Instead of running into his arms and welcoming him home, I froze in place when I heard the door open. He carried a medium sized bag sat it down by the door as he walked in. For a moment or two we stared at each other not knowing what to do or say. Finally, I find my voice and said, "Hi baby, welcome home." He walked over to me and put his arms around me and held me gently in his arms. Slowly he embraced me with a kiss that was just as gentle as the hug. He eased me to the couch and started stroking my hair and touching my skin as if he were blind and trying to feel me for the first time. He touched me from head to toe before he ran his tongue down the length of my body and back up again. This brought back memories of our first special night together. I longed for his touch this past year. I savored every minute of his touch as if it were the last time. I arched my back as he entered me ever so gently. He let out a quiet gasp as my warmth surrounded him. We were one again. We both held out for as long as we could before exploding together in ecstasy. It seemed like an eternity but was only a moment before we caught our breath. I gently rubbed my hands across his chest as the sweat glistened in the light. He moaned in response to the warmth of my touch and we exploded over and over again until we both were spent. I was having mixed emotions and wondered if he missed me or was this just another game. We both drifted off to sleep, not waking until dawn. Dinner was still on the stove.

It was morning and all I had on my mind was getting some answers from Demetrius. I hoped he was ready to answer my questions. I at least deserved that much. He walked into the room where I was sitting. He looked as good as he did when the night he was arrested, a little heavier, but still a good-looking man. I wanted to know why he was selling drugs because the story he gave didn't sit well with me. I knew he would lie to me, but I was hoping for a more believable lie than what he gave. He claimed that he wasn't selling drugs, but was holding something in his car for one of his friends and when the police searched the car they found it. That may have been true, but with his record I doubted it. I went on and on about this until I got tired of hearing it so I decided to drop it for now. I also decided not to reveal to him that I found out about his past because I wanted to see how long he would keep it from me. It was already five years since we hooked up and he had not mentioned his jail and prison time to me at all. What else could he be hiding?

I went on with my day to day routine, going to work and throwing myself into everything that crossed my desk just to keep my mind off my personal situation. Things got back to normal after a while and Demetrius was that kind and affectionate person I met New Year's Eve. He was attentive and loving, who wouldn't accept that? At times, he seemed a little edgy but I brushed it off as trying to get settled in and hoping he would find a job soon. He was even back in church; yes, and in the pulpit as if he had not just spent a year in county on drug charges. Oh, well, I couldn't worry myself about it and I surely couldn't judge him. We were living in sin and that in itself was wrong. We both had to deal with our own demons and I decided that I would work on myself before I tried to put him in check.

In the year that he was gone, I fell into a depression of sorts; not talking or visiting with friends or family. I became a recluse, hiding away in my own little messed up world. Hell, I didn't even read my favorite books. I couldn't remember the last time I played music. I loved my music. At least I used to. I had to be honest with myself. I was ashamed of how my life was turning out and I knew others were talking behind my back. What they were saying was partially true, I allowed myself to be caught up with a bad boy, a thug. He was changing me and I allowed myself to be changed. I had long since stopped going to church and bible study. I had to gain control of myself before I slipped too far away from who I really was.

Before I met Demetrius, I was a hardworking woman, a proud woman who had accomplished a lot and overcame lots of adversity. I finished high school and went directly to college, unlike my peers. After college, I met and fell in love with my now ex-husband. I thought my life had taken a turn for the best. I was wrong, he was a useless pain in the ass, an everyday sorry man. He was abusive; not physically but verbally. He would talk to me as if I were his child or even worse, his servant. He wasn't an affectionate person. When we met, he appeared to be nice and caring but that was not a part of his character. He tried to take away all my self-esteem and make me feel inferior and helpless, but I was too strong to allow him to take away my dignity.

After a year of wedded bliss, I got fed up and filed for divorce. Irreconcilable differences because I knew I deserved better than him. Upon receiving the court date, I started having second thoughts. I started wondering if could I have tried harder or tried a little longer. The sensible voice inside my head told me I was doing the right thing. Well, that court date came and went without any signs of my ex-husband. I guess I was glad because I was the winner by default and awarded the divorce that went into effect two months later. He moved out and I started a new life. I knew in my heart of hears that ordeal would one day be behind me as I strived to do better next time.

I knew I was slipping fast when co-workers and supervisors starting noticing a change in me. One morning after arriving to work, my supervisor called me into her office and asked me if everything was okay. I explained I was having some personal issues and they would be resolved soon. She offered me assistance if I needed any and mentioned that some of the staff were concerned I was losing my grip on my work. I didn't return a few phone calls, or worked on any of my files, that didn't mean that I was losing it, did it? Again, she offered me some assistance if I needed it, she even advised to take a couple of days off work so I could pull myself together. I accepted the couple of days off, cleaned off my desk and started walking to the parking garage.

I was so stressed and worried lately that I didn't notice that I missed my period last month. I certainly hoped it was from stress. I was feeling tired and listless as of late, but I thought it would wear off once Demetrius and I got things squared away. I got in my car, laid my head back on the head rest, closed my eyes and relaxed for a while. I felt myself drifting away and before I knew it, I was falling asleep. I found myself tossing and turning until I woke up fully and looked down at my watch; forty-five minutes had passed and I was till parked in the garage.

I tried to pull myself together, started the car, and backed out of my parking space onto the street. I didn't feel like going directly home so I drove west until I reached the beach. I pulled into the lot and turned off the engine. I sat and watched the waves and they went back and forth away from the shoreline. It was so reviving to sit near the water. It had a calming effect on me. I told myself that everything would be okay, but I couldn't ignore the goose bumps on my arms as I let the thought pass. I sat and watch the water for about an hour before I realized I was hungry. I walked into a burger stand and ordered fries and a shake to go. I returned to the car to nibble on the fries and sip the shake while I watched lovers go by; some hand-in-hand and others laughing and talking while they held each other around the waist and walked on the shoreline. I wondered if Demetrius and I would ever return to the couple we once were before he was arrested. I daydreamed of that for a while before starting up the car again and headed for home.

Chapter 11

When I got home, there was a strange car in my carport so I drove around the block and parked on the street in front of the apartment. I wondered who could be visiting this time of day. I got inside and to find Demetrius' brother. He stood up to leave, spoke and walked out the door. That was strange, why did he rush off like that? I wouldn't have thought twice about it, but Demetrius was acting so strange that I couldn't avoid it.

I asked "what's wrong?"

As he turned away from me he said "my oldest brother was killed in a drive by near my mother's house."

"Babe, I'm sorry. What do you need me to do?"

I immediately reached out to him to offer my condolences, but he didn't accept that very well and turned away from me. I didn't know what to say to him at that moment so I left him to be alone. He was no more a stranger to death than I was because we both buried siblings in the past. I lost two brothers to street and gang violence and so did he. Life is ironic, isn't it? Some people can dish it out, but can't take it. What I mean by that is this family has been known to do their own little dirty work. They have the nerve to think it wouldn't come back around to them and their loved ones. I know their father, a minister of God told them that they will reap what they sow. "Live by the sword, die by the sword"

Over the next week, funeral plans were being made for Demetrius' brother. They were still in shock and taking his death really hard. His poor mother had to be sedated after hearing of his death. It's great they were a very close knit family and they all supported each other during good and bad times. There would be rough times ahead trying to get over this tragedy. They would need to hold each other up and stay strong. It was no surprise for me to find out that his brother had no life insurance and the family had to pitch in and raise the money for the services. I'm sure most of that was likely to come from their illegal activities in the street. The funeral would be held at their father's church where he would deliver his eulogy. To fit in, I offered to write the obituary and they all agreed that I would be good at that. I gathered the information and took notes so when I got home I could type it up. Demetrius was pleased that I offered to help in his time of need. That was the least that I could do since I was a part of the family now.

I sat as friends and family brought food, desert, drinks and flowers to show their love and offer condolences to the family. There is one thing about black people, we knew how to show up and eat and drink when someone is grieving. It's something that can't be explained, it is just that way. It was such a sad time that I had no time to think about what I personally had to deal with in my relationship with Demetrius. All I knew was he needed me and I needed to be there to support him and help keep his head straight from thinking about retaliation on the person responsible for the death of his brother. They were gang members so it was probably rival gangs that committed the drive by.

As the days went by, we spent a lot of time at his mother's house making the final arrangements for the funeral services. I was by his side every day, even though I would have rather been at home with Demetrius. While we were there the mortician called to say the family could come and bring the clothes his brother would be laid to rest in. Demetrius being the brother with the most exquisite taste bought the suit, shirt and tie to take to the mortuary. The suit was a navy blue, three-piece with a pin striped vest with a powder blue shirt with cuffs, he finished the ensemble with sapphire blue cuff links. His brother always wore one earring in his ear so Demetrius added a single stud earring.

The entire family piled into their cars and headed off to the mortuary for the final time before the funeral services. Demetrius handed the clothes to the mortician. We were asked to wait for approximately thirty minutes while they dressed the body. Before the trip to the mortuary, a lot of the family was still in denial, but sitting in the waiting area made reality set in real hard. You could hear everything from silent cries to loud outbursts of grief. Some of the cousins and older relatives were trying to console others, but were hit hard themselves. This caused the wait to become a little too hard to handle. Relatives that were holding on to their strength had to escort others outside for a breath of fresh air.

I too became overwhelmed with grief that I had to step outside for a moment to regroup. The wait seemed to take forever. The family was overcome with grief. If I could make it through this and the final service, I would finally have a chance to get some much needed rest. For some reason, I was feeling so drained and weak that I thought I was coming down with something. I wanted to rush home, take a warm shower and get into bed with Demetrius by my side.

Demetrius took the viewing harder than I thought he would. For a minute, I thought he would pass out, but he caught himself and held on to his brothers as they all cried together. I heard them swearing that there would be vengeance on whomever had done this to their brother. From where I was standing, I thought I saw Demetrius put something in the casket but I wasn't be sure. His brothers were making gang signs with their hands and speaking all types of slang. Even in their grief they held strong to their gang affiliation. To me, this was so sad and tragic, even more tragic than the death of their oldest sibling. I stood back until they finished their viewing, and then I stepped up next to Demetrius so I could view the body. The mortician did a good job. He looked asleep. The casket was steel blue in color. There was a casket spray made of white and blue carnations lying at his feet. It was lined in blue and white satin with R.I.P., his name, date of death and a gang slogan engraved in the center. No one noticed shake my head from at the sadness of it all. I took one last glance and saw the blue bandana I thought I saw Demetrius place in the casket. It was draped over his brother's right hand as if he was holding it. I felt sick to the stomach and asked Demetrius to walk me to the car so I could wait for him. I told him I didn't feel very well and wanted to go home to lie down.

Rossilyn Lillard

We drove home in silence and that was fine with me. I was sickened with the affiliation Demetrius had with the streets and how it influenced his life. His brother was dead and he acted as if it was okay to kill someone else in exchange for that. I quickly stepped out of the car and ran to the door of the apartment with Demetrius following behind. He opened the door and I ran toward the bathroom and barely made it before vomiting all over the place. As soon as I felt like it was over, I would start again. I felt so dizzy, lightheaded and awfully weak. At last, I could get up and make it to the bedroom, but it wasn't easy. Demetrius looked worried. He sat beside me on the bed and held my hands to make sure I was okay. After promising I would stay in bed and rest, he left hesitantly to go back to his family.

It was after midnight when Demetrius came in. He was bumping into tables and knocking over things as he made his way to the bedroom. I got up to see what he was doing. It was dark in the apartment so I thought that was the reason he was making so much noise. It wasn't the darkness he had the problem with, he was drunk. Demetrius, in his grief-stricken state, drank way too much. For him, a beer is too much because he couldn't handle the stuff. I guided him to the bed to prevent him from falling. He leaned back on the bed and fell into a drunken stupor. I don't know how he made it home without falling asleep at the wheel and having an accident. I guess it's true that God takes care of babies and fools. This was surely a foolish move, but I was glad that he was safe and at home.

The next morning when I turned over to reach for Demetrius, he was already out of bed. I got out of bed, washed my face and went into the kitchen. I figured he was there having breakfast or coffee, but there was no sign of him anywhere. I checked outside and didn't see his car either. I wondered when he left and why didn't he tell me that he was going out. I couldn't spend my morning worrying about him. I had to call my doctor's office to see if she had any appointments available. I haven't been feeling myself lately. I thought it was past time for a physical check-up. Great timing on my part, she had an eleven o'clock available. I hurried and got dressed so I could make it on time. It was about a thirty-minute drive to her office so I didn't take the freeway. I took back streets and I arrived about five minutes early. The nurse called my name as soon as I signed in. I followed her into the screening room to have my vitals taken. Afterward, I was taken to an exam room to wait on the doctor. Shortly after me entering the exam room, my doctor walked in. She was your typical young, white, well off type of person, very calm and caring. While she examined me, she asked if I had any health concerns. I told her I was feeling a little under the weather and thought I was coming down with the flu or something. She told me that everything looked okay, but she would run a battery of tests. She took my blood pressure; it was fine and my weight was stable. She told me her nurse would call me in a few days when the lab results were in. I dressed and drove back home. I knew everything would be okay. I was just under a lot of stress lately. This was all Demetrius' fault, his double life and arrest, not to mention all that talk of getting revenge on those that killed his brother.

 I made it back to the apartment and Demetrius still hadn't been here. I checked the answering machine for messages. He left a message around noon to say his was running a few errands. What errands did he have to run before the sun came up? I had a very bad feeling about this; the nervous feeling in the pit of my stomach said I was right. I called his mother but he wasn't there and he had not been there. I prayed he isn't in the streets with his brothers trying to find out who killed his brother. I couldn't take too much more of this. I was a different type of person than he was. I needed to figure out how to end this relationship before I got in too deep.

Demetrius came home later in the evening looking better than he did last night. He came over and gave me a big hug while asking what I cooked for dinner. He must have gone all day without eating because he ate seconds of the chicken, mashed potatoes and green beans I cooked. He had a way of making everything okay with us. He could look at me and I would do just about anything he wanted me to, well almost anything. While finishing up his meal, he remained quiet the entire time. I also ate in silence, but for a different reason. I was wondering where he was all day, but I didn't ask and he didn't tell. I would give him enough rope to hang himself.

After cleaning the dishes and putting the leftover food away, we sat down and watched a movie. He laid on the couch and put his head in my lap. At that moment, we were like a normal couple in love spending quality time with each other. Lately, t, he had not been too romantic. Even when we got into bed, he would give me a quick peck on the lips and fall asleep. I guess the idea of burying his brother was weighing heavy on him and he just wasn't in the mood. Tonight, was no different. We got ready for bed after the movie and he quickly fell asleep. I on the other hand couldn't fall asleep. I was too hung up with thoughts of his brother's funeral services. This would be something to see and I don't mean that in a good way. For their mother and father's sake, I hoped it would go smoothly, but I had my doubts. When you're from the streets and affiliated with gangs, there was no such thing as going smooth. I'm sure the gang family would have their way at this service just like all the others.

I finally drifted off to sleep and surprising enough, I slept all night. I didn't awaken until morning. When I got out of bed, Demetrius was already up sitting in the living room watching television. Demetrius was already up sitting in the living room watching television. Normally we would greet each other with big hugs and passionate kisses, but Demetrius barely looked up to greet me.

"We have a couple of hours before we need to dress for the services. I want to spend some time with you to discuss our relationship." Demetrius never took his eyes away from the television screen.

"Demetrius, I know your brother's death is hard for you. I am here for you. Don't shut me out." He ignored my statement.

"I went to the doctor today. She ran some test and I should have the lab results back in a few days."

"Let me know when you get the results, he responded. Don't worry so much, everything will be alright."

"I feel like you have given up on us Demetrius. We don't talk, we don't' make love anymore and you're never home. What's going on with you?"

Demetrius was thinking on the same lines that I was and thought it was nothing to be worried about.

Chapter 12

This was my opportunity to talk to him about his lifestyle. I was concerned where he may end up. To my surprise, he jumped from the couch yelling at me; shouting obscenities I'd never heard him speak before.

"You're sounding like my ex-wife Arlene. Why can't you be supportive?"

"I am here besides you Demetrius if you would let me in."

"You know I'm going through a lot with the death of my brother. His service is today, but all you can think about is yourself."

"I love you. I'm afraid that you will do something that will send you back to jail."

"You are one selfish bitch. You don't give a damn about me or my family. Shut up and stop talking to me."

"I love you Demetrius, but as long as you're involved in gangs and dealing drugs, you will not be welcomed here.

I've always thought Demetrius was better than his brothers. Most of the time, it seemed he was doing what they did to fit in. I know there is a code in the streets and gang life is not something you could easily walk away from, but with him I always thought he could turn away anytime he chose to do so. He dressed better than they did, he acted differently and he only talked that street shit when he was away from home and church. I thought he was a better person, he worked and was charming. He had me fooled, his good looks, exquisite dress and charming politeness were all things he used to bait women in. After he was in, he did whatever he chose to whether you liked it or not. Why didn't I see all of this coming? Why didn't I let him go when I had the chance, while he was locked up? Love, it was love that prevented me from kissing his ass goodbye and now it was too late.

All of a sudden, Demetrius grabbed me so hard I almost lost my balance. He caught my fall by jerking me back upright and slapping me so hard that I fell to the floor. I reached toward my mouth and felt the blood as it ran down the corner of my mouth. I was so shocked I could not raise myself from the floor. I waited for him to reach for me and say he was sorry, but that didn't happen. He looked at me and said "Bitch get up! I said get up!" The look on his face told me he was furious with me for trying to tell him what he could or couldn't do. "I'm my own man, he said. I will decide when or if we stop being a couple." He turned to walk away. He looked back at me with a scowl that scared the hell out of me. He said, "Now get cleaned up and dressed so we can bury my brother."

Rossilyn Lillard

I got up like he said and went to the bathroom to look at the damage to my mouth. My bottom lip was slightly swollen and there was a small cut in it. I ran cold water on a face cloth and dabbed my lip until there was no show of blood. Now how was I supposed to cover this up? Demetrius walked in the bathroom while I was still looking in the mirror and he turned my face towards his. He kissed the corner of my mouth, my lips and then my neck as he ran his hands down my body. I couldn't believe this man who had just slapped me down was now going to make love to me in the bathroom. He picked me up and sat me on the sink, snatched my nightgown up around my waist and rammed his hardness into me. This was not the loving, kind man I was familiar with, the man that treated me with as much gentleness as you would give a baby; this was a stranger I wished I had never met. I guess all the stress he was under finally came to a head and he released it all in a moment's notice so strong and hard that he violently shook all over. His knees got weak and he sank to the floor. He started crying and mumbled he was sorry for hitting me earlier. Me, the blinded lover bent down to him and kissed his tears away. I wanted to believe he didn't mean to hit me and forgave him instantly.

Too Scared to Run

I was beginning to feel light headed again and had to sit on the edge of the bed. I sat until the feeling passed and then I got dressed for the funeral. Demetrius dressed in a navy suit similar to the one he bought for his brother. I selected a navy suit with a short jacket and topped it off with a cream, knit blouse. I pulled on navy nylons and navy pumps. I looked like the grieving sister-in-law. We drove to his mother's house to wait for the limousine that would drive us to the church.

Chapter 13

His mother looked so small and frail in her grief-stricken state and had to be assisted out to the sidewalk to get into the limo. His two sisters looked nice for a change; they were wearing black dresses, black pumps and black hats that matched the black and white their mother was wearing. The brothers all wore navy suits like the one Demetrius was wearing. I must say they all cleaned up very well. They looked good. The limo ride was slow and quiet except for a few sniffles here and there. We reached the front of the church and there were crowds of relatives and other people standing around waiting to get a look at the family. As we piled out of the car, different people came up to the family to hug and shake hands expressing their condolences while others just stared as we lined up in pairs to walk into the church. We were led into the church by the assistant pastor who read the Lord's Prayer as we walked down the aisles of the church. As the ushers seated each one of us, we could see the casket down front with the lid already opened. There were floral arrangements of various types the sat on each side of the casket along with standing sprays of carnations and roses sent by family and loved ones. The church was packed. People were still arriving after we were seated. The sides of the church were lined with people that waited to be seated. Ushers had to bring chairs from the church annex to accommodate the overflow. I looked around the church to see guys, young and older with rags around their heads, throwing up gang signs with their hands as others from the gang entered the church with no regard for the family during their period of mourning. I noticed Demetrius nod a few times as he looked around the church to see who was there. I tried not to make eye contact with too many just in case the makeup I applied was not doing a very good job. I covered up the cut as much as I could and added lipstick and liner. I couldn't get over Demetrius' temper.

The funeral was beginning and I hoped it wouldn't last all day. You know how we tend to drag everything out for as long as possible as if this would keep our loved ones with us a little while longer. A woman stood up to sing. She stirred up a lot of feelings in the church as she belted out her rendition of "Precious Lord." She had the entire church emotional and in tears. After that selection, someone read a scripture and next someone read the expressions of thanks for the family. Finally, it was time for comments from family and friends. It was announced that comments should be kept to a two-minute maximum. Family and friends took the podium one after the other with their own words of remembrances. Things were moving along swiftly and most speakers kept to the two-minute timeframe. Of course, the gang couldn't miss the opportunity to be seen or heard. A group of them dressed in gang attire with tennis shoes, rags hanging out of their back pockets or tied around their head paid tribute to their fallen family member and vowed in front of the church to seek revenge. This was unsettling on the church. They all threw up their gang sign and returned to their seats. This went on until each of them came to the mic to say whatever it was they had on their minds and to step over to where his mother sat to shake her hand or give her a kiss on the cheek. I saw a few of them put money into her hands as they stepped away from where she sat, throwing a sign toward Demetrius and the other brothers.

Their father, the minister delivered the eulogy in a calm voice at first and then he seemed to turn into someone else as he begged the church for peace and humility. He was directing his message to the gang. I'm sure and he told them vengeance was the Lord's and they should not allow the devil to control their emotions and actions, but to seek guidance from the one and only true leader, Jesus Christ. A quick wave of sound filtered through the church as different ones lashed out at the pastor and his message. It didn't come as a surprise when one of the gang members stood up and told the pastor they would seek vengeance and someone would pay for what they did to their fallen member. Demetrius' father continued to plead with them to let it go, let go of the violence and stop the killings. He reminded the church of how killing others would not bring his son back and how he hoped that his son's death would deter another young man from joining gangs and dying in the streets.

The program moved on to the final selection from the choir. They sang "I'm Going up Yonder", a traditional going home song that brought out all types of sadness and grief from the family. I reminded myself not to judge, but I was sure that this song was inappropriate. When the choir ended their selection, the ushers prepared for the parting view and stood up at the back of the church.

The Deacons of the church stood near the head and foot of the casket to direct the church in the viewing. The ushers asked everyone to stand as each row walked down the aisle to the front of the church to view the body. Some took a quick look while others stood for a while, crying and bending over for a quick kiss or a slight touch on the hand. The turnout was so large that it was a while before the family was ready to get up for viewing.

It started off with family going row by row until it was just a huge crowd of family around the casket. Some were silently weeping while others cried so loud that sound no longer escaped their voices. The gang was ever present, they were considered family. When they viewed the body they dropped money, rags, liquor bottles and beer cans in the casket. Hands waved over the body as if he could see them, making spectacles of themselves. Demetrius was leaning over the casket talking to his brother. I tried to stay by his side, but it was too much for me to handle so I went outside to join others that walked out. Finally, everyone was out of the church and we headed back to the limo to go to the cemetery.

This was the hardest part of the funeral for me and for most families. This was more than one could take. The thought of leaving your loved one behind was hard on anyone. I paid close attention to Demetrius and his gang brothers as they stood and looked down on the casket for the last time. As hard as they were, tears streamed down their faces. It was touching. I felt bad for his mom. She took a lot in her lifetime and to bury her first born son must have been more than she could bear. Her sons helped her to the limo as she tried hard to pull away from the casket that held the body of her child. As the crowd headed back to their cars, Demetrius and his buddies stayed back for a while longer doing only God knows what to that grave. I stood outside the limo and waited until Demetrius returned to the car and then we both got in and sat down. With that behind us, I started to feel sick again and the limo driver had to pull over twice before we arrived back to the repast so I could throw up. One of the sisters looked at me and asked Demetrius if I was pregnant. He shrugged her off and held on to me to be sure that I was okay.

 I was in no mood mentally or physically to sit around his brooding family for the rest of the day. I said goodbye to everyone and had Demetrius take me home. He appeared to be concerned about me and asked if he should stay with me. As bad as I wanted him to, I said that he should get back to his family. He told me he would come home early. That was good enough for me. I undressed, took a hot shower and got into bed. I tried to read a little, but I was feeling a little too light headed to do that so I watched television for a bit. I dozed off around two thirty or so and didn't wake up until around six thirty. I was hungry and wondered if Demetrius would remember to bring food home for me. I decided to call and remind him.

I called his mom's house and someone told me that Demetrius was not there. I asked to speak to his mom. "Hello, this Arlene, is Demetrius there? "No sweetheart, he's not here" she replied. I hung up the phone and waited.

Demetrius came home shortly after with a huge plate of food from his mother's house. I was happy because I was famished. I sat down at the table to eat. Demetrius sat down with me and ate a little something too. He hadn't eaten a lot this past week. I was glad he ate a little. I was just glad he was home with me. I loved this man despite his past, despite his involvement with gangs, he was my Mr. Right. I would do any and everything to keep it that way.

Having the look of sorrow on his face, he touched my lip where it was cut as he sat there and watched me eat.

"Are you feeling alright? Have you heard anything from my doctor yet?"

"I'm still waiting for her call with my lab results." I couldn't go on feeling this way especially, when I had to return to work next week. I had no energy, I couldn't keep any food down and my head was always spinning. I was a mess. This had to end so I could go on with my life.

Suddenly, it hit me like a hammer. I could be pregnant. For a moment, I imagined Demetrius and me as parents to a little boy, fine like his daddy. Demetrius was calling my name while I was daydreaming, but I didn't hear a sound. He called my name again and I snapped out it. He reached out for my hand and held it gently.

I asked him "what's wrong?"

He said "I'm afraid of losing you. If you left me, I would be devastated."

"Maybe your sister was on to something. I might be pregnant."

He was quiet at first. He picked me up and twirled me around the kitchen floor and if this was the best news he ever heard. I was happy because he was happy. We were eager for the lab results.

Chapter 14

The remainder of the weekend went by without anything interesting happening. I got lots of rest. Demetrius appeared to be happy and stayed around the house lounging with me. He attempted to cook dinner, but burned the steaks he put in the oven. We had to order takeout. Later, we watched a movie and fell asleep after a long session of lovemaking. He was as tender as ever, taking his time to please me. In return I pleased him. When we were satisfied, we fell asleep in each other's arms. It was a good thing that we made it an early night because the next day we had to rise early and off to work we had to go. Demetrius was working for a roofing company and doing well these past few weeks. I could see things were looking up for us. We may be having a family soon. We needed to save as much money as we could. I believed Demetrius would stay out the streets if I kept him occupied. I prayed for a pregnancy so my man could be at home where he belonged.

I returned to work immersed myself in my work and I had plenty of it. I passed a few co-workers in the hallway and they welcomed me back and hoped I was feeling better. I did feel a little better. I knew I looked better too. I worked straight through my morning break filing and returning calls to clients that left multiple messages. I found myself feeling good about myself again. My supervisor expressed her joy of my returning full force and expected great things from me in the near future. Sounded like a promotion or at least a little more responsibility.

I usually ate lunch alone, but since I was just returning to work, I agreed to have lunch with the girls from the office. We drove to the marina which was just a short distance away and we all ordered fish or shrimp. It was nice outside so we chose to eat on the patio of the small restaurant. I laughed as they caught me up on what I missed in the three days I was gone. They were nice people and I really enjoyed lunch with them. Arriving back at the office, I sat down at my desk and noticed a message stuck to my telephone from my doctor's office. I assumed my lab results were back so I called to speak with my doctor. She gave me the results of my lab work. I was a little anemic and I was eight weeks pregnant. I could have leaped to the sky when she told me that news. She prescribed prenatal vitamins for me and told me congratulations. I couldn't wait to get home to tell Demetrius the great news. He would be so excited that we were going to have a baby. I didn't take another look at the clock. I worked and worked until quitting time.

I frantically drove home to tell Demetrius the good news. I took the freeway. It had to be my lucky day, traffic was light. I made it home in less than forty-five minutes. I pulled into the carport. As I walked toward my apartment I saw my neighbor, Mike walking out of his apartment. He was working it as he twisted down the stairs. He was something else that Mike. I could take a few lessons from him on how to twist and shake my stuff. I reached the apartment door and it was unlocked. I put away my keys and called out to Demetrius. He stepped out the bedroom with bare chest and boxers on. Damn, he was a good-looking man.

I ran into his arms and told him the good news. He couldn't believe my words. He was far more excited than I could ever be, but I savored the moment as he squeezed me tightly in his arms. We were so excited that we rambled on all evening about what we would name the baby. We talked about moving into a bigger place and he mentioned the unmentionable, getting married. I almost fainted when the words came out of his mouth. We never talked marriage and I guess it was due to neither one of us wanting to rock the boat. Everything was fine the way it was, because we were both married before and didn't want to make that kind of commitment before the pregnancy. I knew he was a good man and he was mine, all mine.

Demetrius went around acting like the town crier telling everyone about the baby. People were shocked that I would have a baby by this man. It was kind of scary if you thought about it, him being from the streets and all. He had a prison record and his family were notorious gang members and very well known. Did I want my child brought up in this type of environment? Would I be able to keep my child on the straight and narrow as he or she got older? Would his or her father pull them over on the other side? That was something I needed to give some serious thought.

During all of this, I forgot all about wanting to get away from Demetrius. I forgot he was contemplating seeking revenge for the death of his brother. I forgot all about the mean side he showed me a short time ago and could only think of our future together as a family. We were having a baby and that changed it all. I would have to come up with a different plan, one that included pulling Demetrius away from his family. He had a strong family bond which I didn't know how to break, but if I came up with a good enough plan, what would the consequences be? His family liked me well enough, but he was still more theirs than mine. I could have a problem if I became an obstacle in their way.

My co-worker was a real estate agent. She talked to me about a first-time home buyers program before. This would be a great time for us to move into our own place. He did mention the apartment being too small for our growing family. I would convince Demetrius we needed to buy a house. It needed to be far enough away from his family, but not too far from my job. I might have to commute longer, but who cares if it would get my man away from those people. This could give us a new start, especially when the baby came. I made a mental note to talk to my co-worker as soon as I made it to the office. I would have her start looking for something as soon as possible.

While I was on this family topic, I would indulge Demetrius in a little marriage conversation. If he was serious about getting married, I would like to do it before the birth of the baby and way before I got too big to walk down the aisle. I hated weddings where the obviously pregnant bride waddled down the aisle wearing all white like she was the Virgin Mary. It was embarrassing and tacky. Thoughts of a fairytale wedding should have been tossed aside as soon as the bride-to-be found out she had a little bun in the oven. I wanted a small wedding with close family and friends only. I wanted it to be elegant and in good taste. I sat on the couch daydreaming for a minute or two when Demetrius stepped back in the room breaking the spell. I would wait a little before bringing up the subject. I didn't want to ruin the afternoon.

For the remainder of the evening, Demetrius and I talked of nothing but the baby and what we would need for its arrival. We decided on making a list of things the baby would need right away and then a list of things to get as it got older. He was so into this and so attentive about everything. This is what made me fall in love with him when we first met, he was so into me and now he was laying it on really heavy. He laid his head on my stomach trying to feel the baby move. I told him that wouldn't happen until much later in the pregnancy. I allowed him to lay there anyway. I finally got to see his silly side when he told me some of the names he was thinking about. We laughed and enjoyed this moment together.

"Were you serious about getting married? I asked. For a second, I didn't think he heard me. He had a blank look on his face so I repeated my question and waited for him to respond. Were you serious about getting married?"

Demetrius stuttered his words when he said "honey, I was caught up in the news about the baby. I got ahead of myself and got carried away. Right now with the baby coming, we should focus on that for now. Marriage can be put on the back burner. I don't think we can afford all of that right now. We should wait until we get better situated to get married." Whatever he meant by that. He went on like this for what seemed hours before he realized that I was no longer listening to him. I didn't know whether to cry or sink into depression after listening to him rant and rave about how we couldn't afford a wedding and how it wasn't a good time. He even mentioned not wanting to give me any old wedding ring, but a carat or two. He told me to wait until after the birth of the baby so I could have a beautiful wedding complete with the ring, dress and whatever else I wanted. Right then is when I turned and walked away from him. I got in the shower and let the water stream down over my tense body while I cried like a baby. I have been known to get myself into messy situations, but this was the worst.

Morning sickness struck me like a bolt of lightning. It didn't ease up until an hour or so later. I tried to eat a light breakfast to avoid being hungry, but that made it worse, so I drank juice instead. I dressed for work without disturbing Demetrius. I couldn't face him after last night. The nerve of him acting like he never mentioned us getting married. I was supposed to be his woman and now I'm having his baby. Why couldn't we get married? Well, we would just have to see who would win this battle. Maybe I would give him an ultimatum, marry me or we could break up, yeah that's it, I would give him a choice. I reached for the door handle of my car and here came Demetrius' hand right over mine opening the door for me.

"What are you doing?" I asked.

He said "How can you leave without waking me or saying something to me before you go to work?"

I lied saying, "I didn't want to disturb your sleep."

"Are you upset over our conversation last night?"

"Upset no, disappointed yes."

He closed my door and I backed out of the carport leaving him standing there with a look of dismay on his face. If he only knew he would have a difficult choice to make, he might have the look of fear on his face instead of looking puzzled.

Rossilyn Lillard

I drove to work listening to the radio to take my mind off the big mess I made of my life the last couple of years. I went from being a divorcee to a woman shacking up with her lover. To make matters worse, I was pregnant with his baby and there would be no ring on my finger. If I was going to give birth to this bastard child, it would be alone. I was deserving of marriage. I wouldn't allow this man to continue dictating how I would live my life. I was tired of doing things his way, even though I was enjoying it until recent. I fell right into his trap and he loved it. He didn't have to think about where I was because he knew I was either at home or work. I gave up everybody and everything else long ago. I was independent when he met me and I would do just fine without him; me and our baby. I had to put together a new plan, one that didn't include Demetrius. I would still look for that house and since it would only be me and the baby, I could move wherever I wanted to. Too many bad memories were unhealthy for the soul. It could wear you down and fast. I had to get out and quick so my baby and I could have a chance at a better life; a calmer more peaceful life.

Chapter 15

I arrived at work and checked my messages. I sorted my work in baskets to respond to important matters first, everything else could wait. I went to my co-worker's cubicle to ask her about finding me a house. She had a few brochures with her that I could take a look at. I looked at a couple of them, but didn't like that the homes were all thirty minutes of where I stay now. I explained to her that maybe I would look away from the inner city for a place. I told her I would get back with her in a few days to see if she's found anything in my price range. In the meantime, she gave me applications for pre-approval that had to be completed. That way, I would know what types of neighborhoods I could afford. I always heard that the further out you bought the lower the cost and the bigger the home.

I returned to my desk to complete the paperwork she gave me. I had to avoid taking them home and Demetrius finding them. I didn't want him to know anything about this move I was planning. If he didn't want to marry, I no longer wanted to shack. I was so embarrassed about my living arrangement that I had long since stopped going to my church. I only went to church on the Sunday he was preaching the sermon at his church.

Even he stopped going to church like he did in the past. Our lives changed drastically and we both allowed it to happen without giving it a second thought.

After a long day at work, I drove home to build up enough courage to give Demetrius an ultimatum. I was sure he wouldn't like the idea of having to make a choice, however, he was leaving me no choice. I went over the conversation again and again in my head until I gave up on it and decided I would just say it. I had a right to say how I would live my life and if a man couldn't respect my decision then he was the wrong man for me. My Mr. Right was turning out to be all wrong. If I get out this mess, it would be a long time before I ever tried my hand at another relationship. I would concentrate on raising my baby the best I could. I may not have been good at relationships, but I knew a little something about how a child should be raised.

Chapter 16

When I pulled into my carport, I didn't see Demetrius' car which meant I had enough time to relax and unwind before having to confront him. I checked to see if there were any messages. There were none so I opened the mail while I sat and watched the evening news. About an hour later, I heard Demetrius come in the door. I didn't wait for him to get settled. I went to him and told him I didn't want to have a child as an unwed mother. If he didn't want to get married then it was best to move out and end our relationship.

I didn't see it coming. I should've known what his reaction would be. He hit me with a backhand so hard, I blacked out. I came to holding and protecting my stomach. I wasn't even showing yet, but by motherly instinct I covered my unborn child. Demetrius pulled me from the couch, pointed his finger in my face and told me, "you are my woman and you better remember that! I will end the relationship when I say it is over, not you!" I cried out I did love him, but I couldn't continue to live this way. I wanted a real family that included a husband.

To get him away from me and out of harm's way, I said to him, "Baby, I'm just all emotional right now because of the baby. I don't want to break up, I just want things to be right with us before the baby is born." Demetrius didn't hear a word I said and came at me again with yet another slap to the face. Then he grabbed me by the hair and brought my face close to his, so close I could smell the anger emitting from his body through his nostrils and mouth. His breath was so hot on my face that it made me wretch. I needed to vomit. I cried out again for him to let me go before I puked. He just held on tighter until I said, "you might hurt the baby." Those words must have gotten to him because he let my hair go and relaxed his hold on me.

I ran to the bathroom where I vomited violently into the toilet. I had to get on my knees and hold onto the sides to keep from falling over. I was sobbing so hard that my entire body felt weak. The pain I felt in my face was unbearable. Unlike the time before, I could tell he did some serious damage to my face. Before I looked in the mirror, I could see the big drops of blood on my blouse, around the floor where I was kneeling and the trail out in the hallway. My face started to feel tight. I knew then my face was beginning to swell. I needed to get some ice, but I couldn't get up yet. I stayed on my knees in front of the toilet long enough for the wretched vomiting to subside.

Too Scared to Run

I struggled to get up from the floor. Grabbing ahold of the sink for support, I raised myself up I catch a quick glance in the mirror, I let out a silent scream and sank down to the floor once again. I sobbed even more violently this time when I saw that one side of my face was so badly swollen that my eye was closed shut. My face was bruised and in so much pain, it was something terrible. I took a towel to wipe away some of the blood that was streaming down my face and that's when I almost lost it. There was a four or five-inch gash on my cheekbone that was laying wide open. Blood was just streaming down my face. That's where the drops of blood in the hall were coming from. I was going to need more than ice this time. I was going to need stitches.

I crawled out into the hallway and called out Demetrius' name but there was no answer. I inched my way to the telephone so I could call the operator. I needed to get to a hospital and this was the quickest way to get an ambulance on this side of town. What a coward he was leaving me there to suffer all alone. How could he do this to me, the mother of his baby? What kind of monster was he to hurt me so badly? What kind of monster would hurt a woman carrying their child?

The ambulance and the police arrived about the same time. A police officer knocked on the door before coming in. He saw me holding a towel to my face and asked the paramedics to come in. They checked me out and had me get on the gurney. I explained to him what happened and that I was pregnant and wanted to make sure my baby would be safe. I gave the officer all the information I had on Demetrius. I told them, I wanted to press charges against him. The officer assured me that he would be arrested and charged with assault. The paramedics carried me to the ambulance and placed me inside the ambulance.

I could see Mike running down the stairs yelling, "Arlene, are you alright? What happened to you?"

He took one look at me and started crying while reaching out for my hand. I asked Mike to follow us to the hospital and he agreed. As he took off to get in his car, an officer stepped in the ambulance to ride with me to the hospital.

The ambulance backed into a space in front of the emergency entrance and the paramedics take me out of the ambulance. Mike is right there by my side as they rushed me inside the emergency room. I started to cry again as the reality of it all hit me hard again. The more I cried the more the blood streamed from the wound on my cheek. I thought of my unborn baby and reached down to grab my stomach as if this would protect it from all harm. I was getting dizzy at the thought of what my face would look like after this assault on me by Demetrius. A horrible thought crossed my mind. What if I lost the baby as a result of this? I would never forgive him for it. He was brutal and I wanted him punished for it.

They asked Mike to wait in the waiting room as they checked me in. The nurse started an intravenous drip, but could only give me Tylenol for the pain because of the pregnancy. A doctor rushed over to me to look at the cut on my cheek. He needed the nurse to wipe away some of the blood so he could get a good look. I heard him mumble something about surgery and sutures. I hoped I misunderstood what he was saying. I was in such horrible pain that at this point I was willing to do anything to stop it, but I had to think of my baby first. The nurse had already attached a fetal monitor and was waiting for a reading of the baby's heartbeat. The doctor ordered the nurse to ice my face for the time being and ordered X-Rays of my cheek to check for broken bones before he could take any further steps.

A technician came in pushing a huge, portable X-Ray machine and started to take pictures of my face one side and then the next. The pictures were developed immediately and the good news was, there were not any bones broken in my face. However, the cut was pretty bad and I would need surgery to put the layers back together to reduce the risk of any major scarring after it healed. The doctor told me a surgeon would be in shortly to discuss with me the surgery procedure and to answer any questions I might have regarding how the procedure might affect my pregnancy and the baby. It would be a few minutes before they took me to the surgery floor, so I asked if Mike could come in. I needed someone to hold my hand. I was so scared, but I knew he would also take my mind off the pain. Mike said to me while they were wheeling me away, "Arlene, you know that I'll be right here when you wake up, girl. Don't worry about a thing. I'll take care of everything."

After recovery and in my own room, I realized that it was all over. I had survived the surgery. I panicked when I realized my face was still swollen and I had really big bandages around my face and head. I cried again. It could have been because of the pain I was in, or because of the entire ordeal I went through. I just didn't know. I called for a nurse to come over so I could ask how everything went. I asked about stitches and she told me that I had to have over twenty-eight stitches to close the layers of flesh in my cheek because it was cut all the way through to the bone. The nurse informed me that when the doctor made his rounds he would stop in to see me and if I had any other questions, he would answer them for me.

Mike came to visit bearing flowers and balloons. He was such a good person. I felt so bad taking up so much of his time. I knew he had better things to do besides running back and forth to some hospital to see me. When he finished fussing with the flowers and all, he had a look of worry on his face. . He told me the police had arrested Demetrius at my apartment. He told me that he was afraid for me knowing the type of person Demetrius was. He said, "Demetrius is going to kill you if you don't get away from him." Demetrius and his family were known for taking revenge out on anyone that stepped in their way and I was no exception. Mike knew I always called him, Mr. Right, but he didn't know he hit me before; at least I didn't think he knew. Mike was just being a good friend. He wanted the best for me. I thought it was a good time to tell him about the pregnancy since; I wouldn't be able to hide it much longer anyway. I liked Mike, he was good people.

"Mike, I'm having Demetrius' baby." He really flew off the handle when I told him.

"Arlene, how could you allow this to happen? That man is not the type of man to settle down with and have a child. He is a gangster, not a family man!" He added, "Well, if you are not that far along I can take you to the clinic to get an abortion; afterward you can tell everyone you lost it, had a miscarriage."

"Mike, I can't do that. I want my baby. I could never have an abortion regardless of who the father was. Destroying a life is not something I believe in. and this unborn child was a living thing growing inside of me. I didn't need to get rid of my baby in order to get rid of Demetrius. I could and would raise my baby without him being in my child's life or mine. This would be the perfect time to make my move and put my plan into action. That's if they keep Demetrius in jail long enough." Mike listened as I talked as if to say, "Girl, you are dumber than I thought you were." It was time for him to leave, but he told me to call him if I needed anything. He hugged me and said "goodbye."

Chapter 17

Not long after Mike left, the doctor came to see me. He told me the surgery went very well and that I shouldn't have too much scarring after it healed. He looked away from me before breaking the bad news to me. He said, "Miss Simmons, I'm sorry to tell you, but your baby didn't survive the surgical procedure. The heart rate dropped too low and the baby stopped breathing." I felt like everything was moving in slow motion. I felt the bed move under my body. I felt like I was falling from a very high place. The doctor continued, "I'm sorry, but your baby didn't make it. The fetus wasn't strong enough to take the stress of the procedure. Again, I'm really sorry." Then the doctor added, "You're young, you will have an opportunity to have other children. Just try to get some rest. You'll feel much better." With those last words, he exited my room. I couldn't cry. I was a strong woman and I've been given bad news before. I could take it. All I needed was time. I pushed the buzzer for the nurse to bring me a sedative and something for the pain that was returning to my face. All I wanted to do was sleep and sleep I did.

I slept through the evening and most of the night until the medication wore off. I felt so overwhelmed with all that went on in my life the past few weeks and months that I was lost as to what my next move should be. I needed to act fast, but I couldn't sort things through like I should have been able to. I needed help, but where would it come from? At times like this, the man in your life should step up and take over, lighten your load. But what do you do when that man was the person causing you the turmoil? I alienated everyone I used to share my life with prior to meeting Demetrius.

My girls used to always be by my side, but we haven't seen or talked to each other in years. I couldn't call on them and expect them to respond to me as if nothing had changed. They knew how my life would probably end up which was no fault of theirs. I just couldn't see it. I was blinded by love or by the thought of love. Being the good friends we were, I would not have expected them to interfere and they didn't. They let the chips fall where they may. I should've been more proactive in my situation before I got in too deep. I should have put up a barrier that only allowed Demetrius to get so far, but I allowed myself to ignore all the warnings and facts just for what I thought would be a world wind relationship. Mr. Right my ass, he was so far from being the right man for me or anyone else as far as that goes. I needed to think fast on what my next move would be. I needed to do it quick in case Demetrius was released from jail. I'll be released from the hospital in the morning. I could think a lot better at home.

I called Mike to see if he could come to the hospital to take me home, but I didn't get an answer. I had to call someone to pick me up but was limited in my options. I called my girl. I had mixed feelings about calling her but I didn't have many other options. The telephone rang three times. I was getting ready to hang up when a voice said, "Hello?" My heart skipped a couple beats. That was a sign of my guilt for not being a good friend. I dropped out of sight and now I was in trouble and needed the very friend I abandoned. In response, I said, "Beverly, is that you?" Immediately all of the years came flooding down on me. I began to cry into the telephone. She didn't say anything, she just held on until I regrouped and found my voice again.

"Everything will be alright." After I blubbered on about what went down.

"I'm in the hospital and need a ride home."

She simply said, "Which hospital are you in?"

Rossilyn Lillard

    She wanted to know how I was doing and I told her to pick me up and I would explain on the ride to my apartment.
    I gathered my belongings and waited for Beverly to arrive. The nurse went the pharmacy to pick up my prescriptions while I waited. Upon her return, she went over my discharge instructions from the doctor. He told me to expect mild to moderate levels of pain and a little stiffness in the face for the next few days. I had a return appointment for the clinic to have my sutures removed. Depending on the damage to my cheek I might also need to see a plastic surgeon for a consultation.
    The nurse grabbed the wheelchair and had me sit down so she could wheel me downstairs to where Beverly was waiting. I was so happy to see her that I started to cry as soon as the nurse helped me into the front seat of the car. She leaned over to hug me after seeing all of the bandages on my face and head and cried with me. We were girls. This is what we did for each other. She asked if I was alright being home by myself. I told her my neighbor, Mike was right next door and would be coming over often to check on me.
    I quickly ran down my story of what happened with Demetrius and me to Beverly.

She was shocked that he had deliberately hurt me. I told her he did something like that before, on a smaller scale. Of course, she scolded me for allowing him the opportunity to hurt me twice.

"Why didn't you put him out after the first time, Arlene?" "This man is evidently as crazy as his brothers. You know they're all in gangs and sell drugs."

"I'm in love with him. I thought it was an isolated incident."

Beverly continued on this path of tearing me down until I could take no more of it.

I cut in saying, "That's not all, I was pregnant, but lost the baby during the surgery. I'm afraid Demetrius is not going to take it very well and he'll blame me for it. But I've got a plan in the makings that will help with that. I have a realtor looking for a place for me. I plan to be out of there before he gets out of jail, hopefully within the next few days." "Do you need help with anything before I leave for work?"

"I'll call you at the office later, if I need you."

Chapter 18

God works in mysterious ways. The phone rang and my co-worker, the realtor found the perfect place for me. She said it was mine if I wanted it. It was a rental with the option to buy. Although it wasn't exactly what I wanted, my current situation made me have to take it. I had so much to do and not a lot of time to get it done. I walked around the apartment for a while trying to get a feel of what I needed to get rid of and what I needed to pack to take to my new place.

I walked into the hallway and had a flashback of that night when blood was streaming down my face and dripping onto the floor. Thanks to Mike, the blood was cleaned from the floors. He tidied up the entire place. He was such a great person. Too bad he was gay. He would have made a great man for some lucky girl. He was compassionate, honest, a good cook and trustworthy. For a second, he was sounding just like Mr. Right. That gave me the chills, so I decided to get busy packing Demetrius' things first. Mike was such a thoughtful person, he had already picked up boxes for me. He anticipated I would need them to pack up this man who deliberately hurt me so badly belongings and he was right. I was finished with him. I wanted him out of my life just as quickly as he came into it. I lost my beauty, my strength and the only attachment I had to him, my baby.

I unpacked the last of the boxes which weren't many because, I decided to rid myself of anything that reminded me of my life with Demetrius. I started to feel a sense of relief moving to a new place. Thinking back over the last two years, I realized I made a mess of my life. Good, innocent Arlene who used to be a good judge of character welcomed who she thought was Mr. Right into her life and look where she is now, running from Mr. Wrong.

My new place is not a part of the city where Demetrius or his family and friends frequented, so I felt safe and confident that he would not find out where I lived. My co-worker knew the standard of living I was used to and because of that, she picked out the perfect condo for me. It was spacious, colorful and on the second floor. Most importantly, it was in a quiet, tree lined neighborhood surrounded by security gates with a 24 hour guard. I'm looking forward to getting settled in my new place and moving on with my new life without Demetrius. After resting, I arranged my closet; clothes first, then shoes and finally accessories. Knowing I would need to keep some consistency and normalcy to get back to my old self. My clothes were important to me. I felt good when I looked good.

I thanked God that my wound started to heal and as promised the scar didn't look so bad after the surgery. However, I still couldn't look too long at my face without thinking about that awful night. I thought he would never stop hitting me. From time to time, I still ask myself how he turned so angry so fast. I was carrying his baby, how he could jeopardize our safety and well-being would remain a mystery to me. If he didn't care about his own seed, I knew he didn't care about the pain and fear he was inflicting on me. Blessings come disguised in many ways and this could definitely be my way out. No baby, no connection and to think I was in love with and wanted to marry this man. As sadness engulfed me, I wept, not only for myself, but for my lost child, my blood. After my tears stopped, I reasoned with myself that I could only go up from here. I was living the single life once again.

I had another week off from work. I took that time to shop for décor for my place. My face was still a little swollen and I'd rather wait a while before driving; besides, the pain medication kept me feeling a little drowsy. I called Mike to see if he was free to drive me around. Of course, he leaped at the opportunity to go shopping. Mike had great decorating skills so I knew he would enjoy spending some time with me and catching up. He would need to pick me up from my new place, because I couldn't risk being seen or followed by anyone on his side of town. He understood and didn't mind at all.

Mike and I shopped until there was no daylight left. I was tired but happy to have had the company. I bought wall hangings, a few rugs, new sheets and comforter sets and pillows. Mike even talked me into buying myself a new outfit for work. Mike picked up a few things for his apartment as well. After our long day, Mike was too tired to drive back home. He made up the couch and quickly fell off to sleep. What a day spent with my friend. I'm really going to miss his being my neighbor now that I'm on the opposite end of the city. No distance is too far for true friends. Speaking of friends, I reminded myself to call Beverly to give her an update on how I was doing. I too drifted off to sleep, but it wasn't a sound sleep.

I was wakened by the sound of the phone ringing and wondered who could be calling me so early in the morning. I closed my bedroom door so I wouldn't wake up Mike. When I said hello, a male voice said he was calling from the District Attorney's office and asked if I was Arlene Simmons. He received my report and asked if I wanted to press charges against Demetrius. Of course, I told him I did. I was afraid and eager at the same time to put an end to this terrible mistake I made in my life.

The DA told me that I was being very brave to pursue this in court. When he told me Demetrius was no stranger to violence against women, I was at a loss for words. Demetrius was arrested numerous times before for domestic violence, but was never charged because the women were all too afraid or intimidated by him and his family to testify. He also told me Demetrius had other assault charges, rape, brandishing weapons and drug charges on his rap sheet. Afraid didn't even start to describe the fear that ripped through my body. I was in shock about the charges I heard about Demetrius. Talk about deception and being fooled by the devil himself. This man was so charming and caring one minute and the next he would go into a blinded rage as if he was two different people. Demetrius was living a double life, but how could this be? He was an ordained minister of God, a preacher, a bible-toting Christian.

I heard enough, but at the same time, I wanted to know more about the devil I allowed to occupy my space, my heart and my home. In addition to those charges, Demetrius was known to be armed and dangerous. The DA explained that if I wanted to put an end to all of the hurt and harm Demetrius inflicted on myself and other women that I would need to follow through and testify in court. If I testified, he assured me Demetrius would get the sentence and prison time he deserved. He also told me to watch my back and protect myself. I needed to be on the lookout for Demetrius or his associates at all times. Before we ended our conversation, he told me in a very serious tone, "Arlene if you don't own a gun you need to buy one. Demetrius was getting released on bail. I needed to stay safe until a court date could be scheduled.

Chapter 19

I took a shower and got dressed so I could fix Mike some breakfast. After the long hours, he put in with me yesterday, he deserved breakfast fit for a king. I scrambled eggs, made grits, bacon and French toast followed by fresh squeezed orange juice. The smell of bacon finally reached Mike's nostrils. He came into the kitchen famished and ready to devour this feast. While we ate, I told Mike about the phone call I had received earlier. His mouth fell open as I went over the charges that were being brought against Demetrius. He was so worried about my safety alone in my condo. I saved the worst for last regarding needing to buy a gun. Mike freaked totally out about it just as I knew he would. I didn't know the first thing about buying or using a gun, so I asked Mike if he knew where I could purchase and learn how to fire a gun. Mike knew of a few places and promised to come on the weekend to take me gun shopping.

Word traveled fast about Demetrius being released on bail. My phone was ringing off the hook with friends and family wanting to know if I was alright. I only allowed a chosen few know where I moved to because I didn't know who to trust anymore. Sad to say, family wasn't exempt. Only those few trusted people were privy to my new whereabouts. I have to admit I'm a little nervous and wondered if Demetrius would try to contact me. If he called, what would he say? What would I say to him? Should I tell him about the baby? So many questions invaded my mind. If he cared about the baby, why did he hurt me? He killed his baby, our baby and if I didn't know any better I would think he tried to kill me too. The weekend needed to hurry up and come, so I could buy some protection.

Each time the phone rang, I answered with nervous anticipation thinking it might be Demetrius. So far, he hasn't called which made me wonder what this silence from him meant. I went about my day dreading putting together my outfits for my return to work next week. I must take extra care of my appearance when I go back because everyone will be looking at my face with wandering eyes forming their own opinions about what happened to me. I only explained my situation to my direct manager knowing it would be kept in the strictness of confidence. Lord knows a nosy woman would do anything to get into someone else's business, so I do all I can to keep my personal life separate from work. I'll need to be very clever with the explanation of what happened to my face to keep the gossip down.

The weekend finally came and Mike was driving me to the gun store to learn more about the best gun for me to purchase for protection. The man at the gun shop had me hold a couple of guns in my hand so I could feel the weight. The first gun was too heavy, so he handed me the second gun which was a blue steel .38. I gripped the gun and the weight of it felt perfect in my hands. I knew this was the gun for me. The man told me it was his best seller to women for protection. On the advice of the District Attorney, I bought the gun and bullets. Now, all I had to learn was how to use it. As it turns out, the man at the gun shop knew of a range nearby where I could get lessons. He even set up my first appointment and told me I would only need to go as many times as it took to feel comfortable aiming and pulling the trigger.

I had just enough time to get dressed and drive down to the shooting range for my first lesson. I grabbed a navy and white sweat suit and my white Ked tennis shoes. I combed my hair back, threw on a baseball cap and out the door I went. Even though it's only a 10-15-minute drive away from my house to the shooting range I was nervous about having a fully loaded gun in my car.

Too Scared to Run

I arrived at the range and checked my gun in while they set up targets for me to practice shooting at. My first few shots came nowhere near the target because I was a bundle of nerves. My shaking hands were proof of that. The trainer stood behind me and wrapped his hands around my hands to help steady my nerves. He told me to aim at the target, take a deep breath and slowly squeeze the trigger. The bullet spent out of the chamber, headed straight for the center of the target and hit it dead on. I closed my eyes and pulled the trigger over and over until there were no rounds remaining in the chamber. I felt myself getting closer to hitting the center of the target each time. I checked out the range, placed the gun back in the glove compartment and headed home. I was feeling a sense of accomplishment knowing I was a little closer at being able to protect myself against Demetrius if I needed to. I wasn't sure if it was beginners luck or if I was a natural, but time would tell.

Sunday morning came quickly, but I couldn't make it to church. I was afraid Demetrius or someone else may see me in my old neighborhood and I didn't want a confrontation. Most importantly, I didn't want anyone following me. It was a mess, but God knows my heart. I would go if I felt safe. I never let anyone stop me from reading my bible though. There was more than one way to serve God. The church is within me. After I finished my reading, I prayed for God to keep me safe through this trial for Demetrius. I normally felt comforted, but I was starting to only feel weary and worry.

I had a lot to accomplish because Monday morning would bring my life back to reality. The past few weeks were a reminder that I forgot who I was. I was a woman with a career, friends and family. I was a happy person who lived my life to the fullest. It was a simple life, but I was happy and fulfilled. I thought I was missing having someone special in my life, boy, was I wrong. That special someone threw my life a curve ball I didn't see coming. I wouldn't in my wildest dreams have imagined my life going down this road.

Being a victim of domestic violence leaves you feeling hurt physically, mentally, emotionally, but most importantly it leaves you betrayed and afraid. I always saw myself as a strong, confident woman who never put too much thought into how others saw me or what their opinions of me were. Now, I feel ashamed and wonder what others are saying behind my back about me allowing Demetrius to get close to me. Even my closest friends feel I was stupid and blame me for my situation. In a way, I agree with them. I made the decision on my own instead of looking to the Man upstairs for guidance. I jumped the gun so to speak and you know the rest. Would I ever be able to forgive myself? Could I trust in my own decisions when it comes to matters of the heart? Love made a fool out of me again.

I went about my day preparing for my return to work including washing and curling my hair. With that out the way, I thought about going out to eat, but decided I would cook something at home. I took ground beef out of the freezer for a meatloaf. I took out potatoes for mashed potatoes. I also opened a can of green beans. That's a well-rounded meal. The remainder would be leftovers for lunch tomorrow. With dinner out the way, I reached for the book I started reading before that infamous New Year's Eve party. It was a good day curled up on the couch. Nothing was going to ruin my last day to relax.

I read a few pages in my book over and over because I kept losing focus and wasn't able to concentrate. Thoughts of Demetrius ran through my mind. I wondered if he felt sorry for what he did to me. Did he toss and turn in that jail cell from guilt and shame before he was released or did he laugh and brag about hitting me to the point that he drew blood? Anger crept in and for an instant I wanted revenge. I wanted to hurt him as much as he hurt me. I wanted him to bleed as I had and I wanted justice for the loss of our unborn child, my child. My child, I couldn't even grieve for my child. I was so busy healing, hurting and moving to process the loss. I knew I would get over the pain of losing the life that was snatched out of my belly, but would I get over the guilt I had for putting my own life in danger. For the first time, it came to my mind that Demetrius had to be told about the baby. There was no way he could find out until I was ready to deliver the news. Would he get angry and blame me, or would he be humble enough to console me over our loss? I couldn't deal with a new episode in my life, I just couldn't.

Chapter 20

I showered and got dressed for work putting on the new outfit Mike forced me to buy. I'm glad he did, at least I looked good, even if I didn't feel good. I was wearing a blue suit, red blouse and red pumps. I was a little hesitant to face my office knowing my nosy co-workers would be whispering and wondering what happened to my face. I took one last look in the mirror and realized I did the best I could with covering the scar on my face. It was still slightly swollen, but overall not as bad as I thought it would be. I had to leave earlier than usual because my new house was a further distance away so needed more time to drive to the other side of town. I locked the door and walked to my car when I suddenly remembered the gun in my glove compartment. I reached over to remove it but thought, what good is having a gun if it's not with me at all times?

Returning to work was easier than I expected. Everyone was understanding and empathetic to my injury. They purposely stayed away from prying questions about what happened to me. I was grateful and went about my day trying to catch up on my work. I wanted to stay busy to avoid reliving the assault. I stayed in my office as much as possible to avoid the stares by my co-workers. They wanted to know what happened, but I would tell in my own time. I brought my lunch from home so I wouldn't need to go out for lunch or even to grab anything from the cafeteria. I was on my grind all week without any uncomfortable confrontations about my time away from work. The week went by rather quickly and by the time Friday came, I was exhausted. I was almost caught up with my work, I made a few new contacts and I was beginning to feel like my old self again.

I was driving home and decided to stop to pick-up dinner. While turning into the parking lot of my favorite bar-b-que joint, I noticed the car pulling in behind me and I thought it was the same car I saw driving near m when I left my office. Probably just a coincidence, so I parked in a space right in front while the other car parked a few spaces down from me. The driver looked familiar. It was a man who appeared to be in his early to mid-30s wearing a dark colored shirt. As he was looking away from me, I stared for a couple seconds because he favored one of Demetrius' family members. There were so many of them it was hard to keep track of who was who. He didn't get out the car and neither did I. I couldn't wait any longer, I was tired and famished, so I got out and went inside to order my food. I was inside no longer than twenty-minutes and as I approached my car, I noticed the car was gone. Why did I stress over the car, that man? The entire situation with Demetrius was slowly taking its toll on my nerves. I exhaled in relief that I wasn't being followed, got into my car and headed home.

After finishing my food, the phone started ringing off the hook. Every few minutes it would ring and then stop before I had a chance to answer it. This happened for about an hour or so. The next time it started ringing, I snatched it up and said hello in a brazen tone to scare anyone on the other end. There was nothing but silence on the other end of the line. Not a sound so I repeated hello but there was still nothing, so I hung up the phone banging the handset against the receiver. This continued until late into the night and then it stopped. Who was calling me and why didn't they say anything when I answered?

In the morning after showering, I made a cup of coffee and stepped onto the balcony to get some fresh air. I could see the main street from there. I had to take a second look across the street when I noticed the same car that pulled into the parking lot of the bar-b-que place parked directly in front of my complex.

Rossilyn Lillard

I wasn't paranoid and this wasn't a coincidence. Someone was watching me, but who and why and how? I took every precaution not to be followed when I moved from my old neighborhood. At this point I wasn't certain this was the same man or even the same car, but it sure did appear to be. I could only see the profile of the person in the driver's seat, but once again, it looked familiar to me.

My heart started to race as I broke out into a cold sweat not knowing what to do or think. I ran back inside and locked my sliding glass door with fear creeping down my spine. Never taking my eyes off the car or the person in the drivers, I reached for the phone to call my girl, Beverly. She would know just what to do to get me calmed down. When she answered, I asked her to come over as possible and I would explain what's going on when she arrived. While I waited, I thought the more the better so I called my old neighbor and dear friend, Mike, to come over too. Seconds turned into minutes, it was taking forever for them to get to me. I kept checking to see if the car and driver were still parked across the street. It had not moved from its parking space. After a few hours, the buzzer rang and I gasped with fear wondering who it was. I peeked out the balcony window and was relieved in a weird kind of way that the car and driver were still in place. I answered the door for Beverly and Mike. I snatched them both through the door and guided them to the couch where I explained everything beginning with the car following me yesterday and ending up parked across from my balcony today.

    Beverly and Mike agreed that someone was stalking me and I was right to feel afraid. After all that has happened in the past, it was safe to say this was the work of Demetrius. It made sense now, the person probably followed me from my job, to the parking lot of the bar-b-que place and then without my noticing, followed me home. I thought I was being careful, but I've been outsmarted. Demetrius knew where I worked so it was a piece of cake, for him to have someone follow me from there. I was leading the devil right to my door.

    Beverly had me call the police to file a report, but they needed a better description of the driver and the car license plate number. I was afraid to go out of my door so I asked Mike to go out and get a closer look. They couldn't do anything about the car because there had been no crime committed so there was no real proof I was being stalked. The officer advised me to be mindful of my surroundings or any strange activities and to call back if I see the car following me again. To hurt me the way he did definitely proved there was no love, just an obsession he had with me. I was his property, he owned me and he believed he had the right to put his hands on me. Why did he care where I went and who I was spending my time with now? What was his purpose in having me stalked, was it to get revenge for pressing charges and sending him to jail? Was his plan to finish what he started and end my life?

I had not heard from Demetrius since he was released from jail. For all I knew, he could have been the person calling and remaining silent on the phone. I tried to chalk it up to a wrong number, but the calls felt eerie. He surprised me by not trying to contact me, but something in of my gut was telling me this was the calm before the storm. Beverly, Mike and I sat around for a while eating snacks. They tried to tell me everything would be alright and not to worry. I had no choice but to worry because I didn't know what Demetrius' next move would be. I kept checking to see if the car moved, but it was still parked across the street. I checked one last time and noticed the car was still in the same place but the driver was no longer in the car. I looked up and down the street as far as I could see, but he was nowhere in sight. Was I letting my nerves get the better of me, convincing myself I was being followed? My complex was gated and you must get past security to enter the grounds. The unit you're trying to access had to be alerted prior to allowing visitors to enter if they had no gate code.

While the driver was away from the car, Mike ran out and wrote down the license plate number and took a photo of the car. If only I could get a better look at the driver. I would feel more secure knowing if he wasn't a friend or family member of Demetrius. My loaded gun was in the glove compartment of my car, how could I get it without being seen if I was being followed by a stalker? Night was quickly approaching and I didn't want to stay in my place alone. My girl had to leave, but Mike was going to stay the night with me. He was such a great, dependable friend. I didn't want him in any danger though. This was my mess and I needed to figure my way out of it.

Mike and I finally drifted off to sleep curled up on opposite ends of the couch. My sleep was restless. Every sound I heard made me jump up from the couch. I tried sleeping, but couldn't. Not only from the discomfort of sharing the couch with a grown man but also out of fear. I was still thinking about the car and driver. I felt uneasy because I believed I was being followed. As the light of day came shining through, I made coffee to calm my nerves. Mike was still curled up on the end of the couch sleeping. I knew he would be leaving soon so I took advantage of him being there and took a shower. So if anything happened, he would be here to help.

I felt refreshed after my shower so, I get dressed for the day. I had no plans but I put clothes on just in case. Mike was awake and looking out across the balcony. The look on his face told me he was looking at something or someone. I got to the balcony and looked across the street, low and behold, the car was still there and the driver was back. I was able to get a better look at the man. I'm almost 100% sure he was the same man from the parking lot of the bar-b-que joint. I knew his face from someplace, but I couldn't recall. I told Mike and he looked at me like a big brother and said "You need to watch your back Arlene. That man is definitely following you." Demetrius may not have contacted me personally, but I knew this was his way of letting me know he had eyes on my every move.

Chapter 21

I went through the morning with my usual routine preparing for the upcoming work week. I went through my closet matching up suits with blouses, pants with sweaters and decided on which shoes to wear with each outfit. I had a few clients to meet with and I needed to look as professional as possible. After settling my wardrobe for the week, I washed a few loads of clothes, prepared dinner and settled in to read a few chapters in my book. As soon as I got into my book, the phone rang. Before I could answer it stopped. When I sat back on the couch it started ringing again, but soon as I answered the caller hung up. Could this be Demetrius calling to check if I was at home? Was this the man parked across the street calling? My mind was bringing up all types of thoughts. I had to stop taking nothing and making it into something.

I read my book for hours until I grew bored. For a while my mind was off the car and everything appeared to be normal. I eventually walked to the balcony, looked across the street and noticed right away the car was gone from its parking space. I took a chance and went outside to look around. The car nor its driver were anywhere in sight. I was relieved walking back toward my unit until I saw a man walking toward me with his head slightly tilted downward. He wasn't a tenant here and I had never seen him around here before. I totally freaked out and went back toward the street when I saw my neighbor run out to the man and hug him. He knocked on her door and she didn't answer so he was leaving. I was such a mess. I hurried inside and locked my door.

The good part of it all is the car and its driver was gone. Thank you, Jesus! I was aching for Sunday so I could attend my church service. It's been months since I last heard a sermon from my Pastor. After hurting me, Demetrius wouldn't dare come to my church. I would take the chance and go in the morning. I would be careful not to drive my old route to church. I missed my old neighborhood, but my new neighborhood was safer and quieter.

I was excited to be attending church. I did what I could to cover my scar and then dressed for t service. I needed to run down front when it was time for altar call to pray for a miracle that Demetrius didn't end up killing me for pressing charges against him. I took one last look in the mirror and left. I went down the stairs that led to my parking space, but not without glancing across the street first. I drove the back way to my church and was especially careful to watch other cars around me before pulling into the parking lot. Before getting out my car, I looked around for anything or anyone suspicious, but I didn't notice anything.

I walked into church and was greeted with love and expressions of empathy over what happened to me. I was seated near the middle of the church surrounded by members I've known for many years. I felt the love they had for me and an overwhelming calmness came over me as the choir marched down the aisle and the Pastor walked up to the pulpit. He glanced at me for a few seconds with a smile of endearment on his face. The choir continued to sing as they made their way to the choir stand. I took a moment to look around the church to see who may have walked in after me.

Service started and the prayer list was read. I was still on the list but they acknowledged me and welcomed me back. After a couple songs by the choir, it was time for the sermon. The pastor asked everyone to stand as he prayed about thanksgiving and forgiveness. Was he telling me to forgive Demetrius? I praised God anyway and was genuinely grateful for Him sparing my life even though I lost my child. After service, I talked with a few of the members as I made my way to the Pastor near the pulpit. We hugged and greeted each other. He told me that I was missed. He also told me to be careful because a couple strange visitors asked about me and wanted to know where I moved to.

Leaving church and walking to my car, I noticed the same car that was parked across the street from my balcony in front of the church. The driver had his head down and didn't see me. I hurried to my car and reached inside of the glove box for my gun. If I was being followed, I was certainly going to be ready if I was approached by anyone. I pulled out of the south end of the church parking lot and turned right to avoid the driver seeing my car. I prayed for forgiveness for bringing a gun to church.

It wasn't the church exactly, but church property. I sped off with wondering thoughts of who could have been looking for me at the church. Something told me the driver of this car had something to do with that. He knew where I lived, but didn't appear that he knew my unit number.

I got home in little to no time, but before I slid my gate key, I circled the block to check for the car anywhere near by building. After feeling safe, I slid my keycard, entered the property, pulled into my space and took the stairs to my unit with my gun in my purse. I got inside and opened the balcony door so I could see passing and parked cars across the street. I took off my church attire and threw on a lounger so I could prepare dinner.

I took a chicken out the freezer before leaving for church and it was ready to be cooked. I seasoned the chicken, cut up some vegetables around it and put it in the oven. I made cornbread, mashed potatoes and to complete this meal, I made a pitcher of grape Kool-Aid. While my meal was cooking, I made a couple of calls to check on Beverly and Mike. I also wanted to give them an update on what's been happening all weekend including my church visit. Mike insisted that I not come back to the old neighborhood until after the trial. He was afraid for me, but my girl Beverly thought it was okay if I went to church as long as I watched my surroundings. I was torn and not sure how to handle this situation. They both loved me like a sister and I knew they wanted me to be safe first and foremost.

After dinner, I cleaned the kitchen and put the leftovers away. I would be able eat from this meal all week. The weekend went by so fast and now it was time to prepare for the week. I reflected over the past year and wondered if I would ever fully recover. I have so much to offer, but I never receive what I give out. I love hard, but always seem to get hurt in relationships. What was wrong with me? Was I too gullible, too loving, and too giving? If this was so, was it wrong to be the way I was? Why couldn't I be respected for who I was and why did I always ask myself why? I knew one thing, I was tired of men taking advantage of me and using me as a pawn in a chess game. It was time for me to show them what I was really made of. It was time for me to stand up for myself and give myself a fresh start.

Monday after I got to work, I made a few calls to see if anyone heard anything from Demetrius. He was staying out of sight. He hadn't tried to make contact with me. Court was in a few weeks so I was beginning to feel nervous and stressed. Thoughts of seeing Demetrius made me both angry and anxious. He would learn our baby didn't survive the trauma he inflicted upon me. I wondered what his reaction would be.

The DA called me to go over the charges Demetrius was facing and again asked if I wanted to follow through with the case. Of course, I said I did. He needed to pay for what he did to me and our baby. I wanted him in prison where all monsters belonged, especially those who put their hands on a pregnant woman. He deserved time behind bars. The DA created a file that contained the police report, emergency room report and pictures so he could show the court to support my case. Along with this he had a long list of charges from Demetrius' rap sheet including gang affiliations and drug distribution. All of which would prove he needs to be taken off the streets.

My supervisor called me into her office to let me know there was a man sitting in the parking lot. She asked if I knew him. I peered out the window and immediately started to shake uncontrollably. It was the same man, the same car that was following me. Demetrius had to be behind this, but what was his point in having me followed? Was he trying to scare me, if so, it was working, I was petrified. First, he harassed me where I lived and now at my workplace. This has got to end.

I called the police to report the man in the car but, once again they told me no crime was committed so they couldn't do anything about it. I told the officer he was trespassing on private property and had no business with us; it was at that point he decided to send a car out. After about twenty minutes, a patrol car pulled into the parking lot, he got out came inside to talk to me. I told him, I already called about the same man being parked across from where I lived. I knew this couldn't be a coincidence.

I watched out the window as the officer went into the parking lot and approached the car. He went to the driver's side of the car, looked in, turned and walked back to my office.

He said, "ma'am, there is no one in the car."

"I saw a man sitting in the car earlier. He was the same man parked in front of my condominium."

"What can I do to stop this man from following me?" I rushed outside to look in the car and sure enough, the man was nowhere to be seen. He told me it was not illegal for someone to follow me, however, if they planned to harm me then it's illegal.

I went back to my office and checked my gun. I wanted to feel the safety of it in my hand because I may need to pull that trigger one day. Throughout the day, I went to the window hoping I could get a good look at the driver of the car, but he was nowhere in sight. Where could he have gone? Why was he parked here? I was a bundle of nerves as it got closer to the end of my work day. I would be getting off soon and didn't want an encounter with the man in the car. I didn't want him to see me leave.

While walking to my car, I looked toward where the car was parked, it was gone. I was relieved that I wouldn't be followed. I got in my car, locked the door and instead of putting my gun in the glove compartment I sat it right beside me. If I needed to use it, I would have quick access. I took one last look in the mirror and pulled out the parking lot. On my drive home, I listened to music on the radio and started to feel myself relax. My life was very stressful and I had long forgotten what it felt like to come and go without looking over my shoulder.

Rossilyn Lillard

Chapter 22

A few blocks from my house, I noticed the car was driving strange. The steering was off so I pulled over to the side of the street. I got out to look at the tires and what luck, a flat tire. I opened the trunk to get out the spare and jack so I could change the tire because I couldn't afford to wait around for a tow truck. I took off my suit jacket and threw it on the back seat of the car. I was bending down to place the jack under the car. I heard someone ask "do you need any help?"

I was relieved I wouldn't need to get all sweaty changing the tire myself. I could change a tire though. My father taught me how to do some things for myself in case there was no man around. I stood up and looked right into the eyes of the man who was following me.

"No thank you. I can do it myself."

I attempted to hide my fear when he reached out and took the jack from my hand. He made small talk and by his demeanor, you wouldn't know he ever saw me before. I talked as little as possible but enough so he didn't suspect anything. He never mentioned his name and neither did I. He had the flat fixed in no time and the old tire placed back in the trunk.

"How much do I owe you sir?

He said "No charge ma'am."

He walked off without saying another word. If he was in a car, it was not parked nearby. I drove away with mixed feelings about the man. Did he flatten my tire just to get close enough to me? How convenient that I get a flat and he just happened to be a passerby offering to help me?

I was left puzzled by the man who was following me. If he worked for Demetrius, why didn't he said anything to me? He went to work on the flat, fixed it and walked off. I hated the feelings I had about this man and often wondered if my imagination was getting the best of me. Is it possible none of this ever happened? I needed closure from Demetrius and the double life he was living. He had me all tangled up in a web of lies and deceit. I wanted to be free of him once and for all.

Sitting in a courtroom in front of Demetrius was going to be difficult. I was hoping to have heard from him long before this so I could see where his head was at. Without so much as a word from him, I had no way of knowing if he was angry at me for pressing charges. He had no right to be angry, but this didn't mean he would not be. Maybe "D" as he was called in the streets would be upset and the man I fell in love with would be remorseful.

I suffered emotional and physical trauma as a direct result of him losing his temper. The wrong words coming from my mouth changed the course of our relationship and now I was very afraid of this man. Somehow something on the inside was telling me I have unleashed my worst nightmare. When Demetrius learns I'm no longer pregnant with his child, he may explode. The guilty always try to place the blame on the other person and refuse to accept responsibility for their own actions. He had no one but himself to blame for the loss of our baby. He would just have to accept that. If he hadn't put his hands on me, he wouldn't be going to trial and I wouldn't be forced to testify against him. I lost my baby and the man of my dreams, I'm scarred for life. Love shouldn't hurt.

Demetrius was playing with fire pretending to be a man of God all the while being a man hustling out in the streets. He shared the pulpit with other ordained ministers, preaching to the church on Sundays knowing he was living a double life. That was crossing the boundaries of deceit as far as I was concerned. That was close to being blasphemous. God was a jealous God and the bible teaches in Matthew 6:24, No man can serve two masters. For either he will hate the one and love the other, or else he will hold on to one and despise the other. Ye cannot serve God and mammon.

Demetrius was the lowest kind of man, he was a wolf in sheep's clothing. I was swept off my feet when I met him because of his perceived Christianity. Did he love God or was this just a front to mask his street life? He was a known gang member in his neighborhood, dope dealer and now to add to the list of his criminal activity he would soon be convicted of domestic violence and a baby killer.

I heard of terrible stories of what happens to men in prison when they are labeled as rapists and abusers of women and children. They are beaten to the brink of death, raped and tortured by the other inmates. I'm not wishing this on Demetrius, but he deserves to be punished for what he did. How could he pull off living this double life? Surely there had to be at least one member of the church's congregation who knew who he really was. Did they not care enough to tell the pastor about his reputation or were they too afraid of him and his family to say anything?

The closer it got to the court date, the more I questioned if I was doing the right thing. I knew in my heart I had to testify so

Rossilyn Lillard

Demetrius would be taken off of the street. He was dangerous and capable of anything. The word on the street was when one member of the family was in trouble they all take on the fight. I'm losing my nerve in fear of retaliation if he gets convicted and sent to prison. I wanted blood right after leaving the hospital, but now I am not so sure. I pray every night that God lead me in doing the right thing. I want revenge, but I have to leave it up to the Lord.

Chapter 23

The knock on my door snapped me back into reality. It had to be a neighbor because the security station did not alert me that I had a visitor. I looked through the peek hole and there was Demetrius standing there as if he was invited. He was standing tall with his hands behind his back. I could not help but notice how impeccably dressed he was. I wasn't surprised at his pop-up visit. It all started coming together for me now. The man in the car who was following me led Demetrius straight to where I lived.

He couldn't see me through the one-way glass in the peek hole, but his expression told me he knew that I was looking right at him. He waited patiently never changing his position in front of my door. I wanted to run and call the police, but I knew if I did he would be gone before they arrived. He would keep returning until he got what he wanted. Plus, I was too scared to run at this point. I decided to let him in. Before I did, I grabbed my gun and put it behind the pillow on the couch. If he tried anything, I would use it. I backed away from the door and waited for him to knock.

He knocked again with more urgency than he did before. I knew that I had to let him in. I wouldn't continue living in fear. I opened the door and he walked in closing it behind him. The apology came without any hesitation.

He said, "Arlene, baby, I didn't mean to hurt you. I don't know what came over me. I love you. I'm sorry. Please forgive me. I love you so much and I want us to be together. I want us to be a family again, you, me and the baby." I never responded. I stood there, watching and listening to him beg me and plead for forgiveness. Hot tears spilled over my eyes and ran down my cheeks, staining the red top I was wearing. I couldn't find words to express what I was feeling. He dropped to his knees in front of me as tears welled up in his eyes. I wanted to run past him and out the door, but I was frozen in place. He mumbled words that were no longer coherent as he reached for my legs and buried his head as a young child would do holding onto their mother.

All the emotions from the night he hit me came upon me and I screamed as loud as I could, "how can you tell me you love me after hurting me so badly!"

He got up from his knees and stood in front of me. For a few minutes, I thought he was going to hit me so I braced myself. In almost a whisper he told me he loved me. He told me he understood why I pressed charges and that he didn't blame me for anything. He told me he needed some type of counseling because he never wanted to hit me again. He blamed his anger on grieving over the death of his brother and the thought of losing me sent him over the edge. He told me if getting convicted and spending time in prison would convince me he was sorry then so be it. I calmly walked over to the door and asked him to leave. He followed behind me without looking back. With tears still in his eyes, he left.

It was at that moment when the door closed that I could breathe. I was light-headed and not thinking straight. I sat on the couch to think about what had just happened. An Academy Award performance is what happened. Demetrius dropping to his knees in front of me was just a sham. He tricked me once but I won't be fooled again. I was going to testify at his upcoming trial and he would go to prison.

Thinking back to my hospital stay, neither Demetrius nor any of his trifling family came to visit me or see how I was doing after my release. Cold hearted and selfish is what Demetrius was. He was only looking out for himself. He didn't ask how the pregnancy was going. Maybe he knew I lost the baby and was just testing me to see if I would tell him first. Well, I didn't say anything about the baby and he would find out in court if he didn't already know. I'm going to continue to ask God for strength and for protection. If I had to move again, or run for the rest of my life, I was going to get justice for me and my baby.

I thought about my estranged family and a sense of loss washed over me. I had brothers and sisters I haven't seen in years. We all lived in the same surrounding areas. My parents were deceased and over the years following their deaths we all separated, living our own lives. I missed my family and wondered where I could run if I needed to. I would like to think if I needed help that at least one of them would welcome me in. If one of them called me today and needed a place to stay, I would open my door with love. Not everyone felt the same way and that was hard for me to digest. During my childhood, I always saw us close knit as we grew into adulthood. Things don't always go the way we believe they would. There was no hatred between any us. We just did not stay in contact like we should. I only had the support of Mike and my girl Beverly for the time being. They were like family and without them I would be so alone.

Before leaving for work the next morning, I visited the security station at the entrance to my complex. I wanted to file a complaint that somehow Demetrius was able to get past them and to my unit without being announced. The Security guard was baffled and told me he didn't see anyone come through the gate walking nor in a vehicle. Well how did he get in, I asked if he scaled the brick wall which has pointed spikes on top? I left there frustrated and feeling unsafe. I moved in a few months ago, choosing this complex because it was gated with security. If Demetrius was going to make this a habit, I would pack up again and move to a new location.

I called Mike on my drive to work and told him about my unexpected visit from Demetrius. He couldn't believe what he was hearing and asked if I was alright. He worried about me so much and I loved him dearly for it. I was scared to death, but didn't let Mike know. Now that Demetrius knows where I live, he could pop-up at any time. He could follow me wherever I go and see who I was with. I didn't believe any of what he said to me and knew he would return. If he wanted to hurt me or have me harmed in any way, he could've done that. He wasn't a stupid man and was waiting until after the trial. He's trying to sway me into believing he's this innocent man who loves me but allowed his temper get out of control.

My co-workers still whispered behind my back and smiled in my face.

What was wrong with these people? I am not the first victim of domestic violence around the office. Six months ago another staff member on the second floor was stabbed by her estranged husband. She survived. When she returned to work they treated her like she had the plague or something. Just like her, I am beginning to withdraw myself from being around any of them unless it's absolutely necessary. I ate in my office, spent breaks in my office and didn't attend any office functions outside my office.

Demetrius called me when I got home from work. Hearing his voice over the phone was unnerving.

"Hello, Arlene, don't hang up."

"What do you want Demetrius?" I asked.

"Have you given any thought to what I said?"

I didn't want to have any discussion about him being sorry because I didn't believe a word he said so I hung up on him. He called back to back every five to ten minutes to the point I took the phone off the hook. This gave me a flashback to the times when the phone would ring, but the person on the other end wouldn't speak. It was Demetrius and I knew this as well as I knew my own name. First thing tomorrow I'm calling to change my number. I would only give it out to a select few people. Demetrius isn't the kind of person who would give up. He would continue until he got what he wanted.

My nights were so long lately. In the mornings, I would feel beaten and tired. My mind was restless and I couldn't focus on my work during the day. I needed to make an appointment with my doctor. Hopefully he could prescribe something to help me relax and sleep at night. It was time for a follow-up anyway so he could check my scar to see how it was healing. I needed to getaway and escape my reality. I could pretend my life was perfect and that I didn't have a care in the world.

Chapter 24

Getting out of bed and dressed was a chore; I had no get-up-and-go about myself. I dragged myself out of bed and into the shower. The hot water did its job and now I was wide awake. I stepped out the shower and was drying myself off when I thought I saw a shadow pass my window. I shrugged it off and walked into my bedroom to get dressed. Then I heard a noise outside. The sound was coming from my balcony. I stood still and quiet so I could listen for more sounds, but it was all quiet. I had to know if someone or something was out there. I slowly twisted the blinds open just enough to peek out and I saw a cat walking around. The cat knocked over a planter when he jumped on my balcony.

I put on a pot of coffee and made toast for a light breakfast before leaving for work. I had a little extra time so I grabbed the newspaper from outside the door and looked in the rental section for apartments. I knew the day would be coming where I would need to move again. I walked down the stairs to the garage where my car was parked and saw Demetrius leaning against my car. My heart stopped when I saw him. He looked up and saw me turn back and ran over to me calling my name.

"Arlene, wait! I'm not here to hurt you. I just want to talk, but you won't answer my calls."

"Demetrius, if you don't leave, I'm calling the police. You don't belong here."

After I threatened to call the police, he turned and walked away. I got in my car, locked the doors and drove out of the garage. I saw no signs of him anywhere. I wondered how in the hell was he gaining access to the property. He was nicely dressed, so I didn't believe he was scaling walls or jumping over gates to get inside.

I had to figure this out and fast. When I first met Demetrius, he would appear out of thin air. Now he is just showing up at my door and in the parking garage. I can't have this. I'm reporting this to the police. He was trespassing on private property and needed to be stopped. It's enough that he has a trial coming up soon, why would he want to add charges? I needed to have the security team looked at because maybe one of them knows Demetrius and is letting him in. He must be paying someone off or something. It's disheartening that he can access me on private property at any given moment. He could be pretty scary so he might be putting the squeeze on one of the guards. It's my intention to get to the bottom of it because I don't like it one bit.

We didn't get many new clients around this time of year so I had plenty of time to look for apartments and condos. I circled a few in the paper and made plans to go see them after work. After browsing the classifieds, I made the call to have my number changed. The numbers available in my area weren't easy to remember so I took what I could get. Those annoying calls from Demetrius had to stop so this would remedy that. I was acutely aware the number change wouldn't resolve the fact he knew where I lived and he came and went as he pleased, but I had to start somewhere.

I drove to the police station during my lunch to speak with one of the detectives. I told him about the pending case I had on Demetrius and how he had someone follow me to find out where I lived. He took one look at his records and told me to be careful because he was dangerous. I asked what I could do about him trespassing on the premises where I lived. Legally, the only thing I could do was take my issue up with property management and let them work out the kinks. I decided to take my court papers and order of protection to management so they could be on the lookout for him on the grounds. I don't know why I didn't think to do that leg of work in the first place.

I called the property management and told time I could bring my court documents over after work. They told me they would help and launch an investigation into Demetrius having unwarranted access to the property. I mentioned that I thought one of the guards was allowing him entrance. I had no proof but it was just a haunch.

The day took what seemed like an eternity to end. I was ready for the door when my girl Beverly called. She asked me if I could come by her house before going home. I tried to get out of her what it was all about, but she told me that I needed to hear this in person. I didn't know if I should be worried or excited about the news she had to tell me. She sounded serious, she wouldn't give a hint or allow me to guess.

When I pulled up in the driveway, I could see Beverly standing in the door with her arms folded across her chest. I went inside and she started pacing the floor. I stopped her and asked what was wrong. She looked at me and told me Demetrius came by her house asking her questions about me. He wanted to know what I was doing and if I was seeing someone else. Beverly told him that I was off work trying to recover after being released from the hospital and had recently returned to work. She paused and then let the main reason for asking me to come over come out. He wanted to know how the baby was and how many months along I was.

Beverly was so nervous because she told him the baby was fine and guessed that I must be at least three or four months now.

"I'm sorry for talking to him Arlene. I didn't know what else to do. I had no other choice."

Consoling her I said "Beverly calm down. It's okay. I would have done the same in this situation. I'm not upset with you. I'm mad at Demetrius. How dare he harass you?"

He must've known something was up. Even at three or four months, I would be showing some. He must have noticed when he came to my place that I didn't look pregnant. He never questioned me about the baby so why ask Beverly?

Maybe I should call him and tell I lost the baby and face the music instead of waiting for the court date. In the courtroom, I would have the protection of the bailiff, but outside of the courtroom I would be on my own. If I gave him the news I would have to sleep with my gun in my hand for fear of him breaking my house in and finishing what he started months ago. I would wait for court and pray he would be sentenced and taken away. By the time he would be released he would have forgotten all about me and the baby.

Several days and nights passed without Demetrius calling or popping up. Maybe he got the message that I didn't want anything else to do with him and his criminal life. I was Miss Goody Two-Shoes and should never have fallen for him so easily. We're not cut from the same cloth, but if I kept dealing with him I would end up being no better than him. I'm not trying to judge him, but even a blind man could tell we're not compatible and that he was no good for me. After being around another person for so long it's easy to pick up their characteristics and habits. Before long, I would be smoking, drinking and doing who knows what else. He sold drugs and possibly used them too. That's the one thing I feared most.

Living a double life had to have its pitfalls. Hiding when he saw someone from church or ditching and dodging the street gangs when he was all dressed up in his church clothes. I often wonder if he does the church thing to make up for all of the sinning out in the streets. What did he want with a little church girl like me? Did he see me as someone he could control and walk over? I would show him just the kind of person I was.

I called the management company to ask about the investigation and they have found out how Demetrius was able to access the property. The manager told me there was a new security guard named Calvin Edwards, hired over the past few weeks who may not have followed policy regarding visitors. I asked if the new guard was abreast of the situation and if he would need a picture of Demetrius. I walked to the security station to meet with the guard and got another shocker. The guard was the man who was following me all those weeks. The same man who changed my flat tire.

Chapter 25

Demetrius found a way to infiltrate my condo complex and gain access to keep tabs on me. He moved a man in complex and would be able to come and go as he pleased. That damn man was making it harder and harder for me to hold onto my religion. For the hell of it, I took a picture out of my pocket and showed it to the man, he shook his head from side to side as if he had never seen Demetrius before. I asked him if he knew or ever saw him before and he denied giving him entrance onto the premises. The manager asked the guard to recite the policy allowing visitors' entrance. He did, without leaving anything out. As I was walking away, I looked over my shoulder to catch the man staring at me so hard, I felt threatened.

I hurried back to my unit and leaned against the door wondering how far Demetrius would go to watch my every move. It's time for me to come up with a back-up plan. I had my gun with me at all times, but I needed to get out of here. How could I move out with his spy at the entrance of the gate? I had to think of a way out. How could I hide a big moving truck on moving day when I found a place? There was one entrance and exit and it just so happened to be by the security station. The other exits were not large enough for a car or truck to enter through. I would plan my move around the schedule of Demetrius' inside man. How? I didn't have that figured out yet, but I would.

I had a lot to figure out before Demetrius found out I was no longer carrying his child. I am not an actress and couldn't fool him into believing I was pregnant. I refused to lie and stuff my clothes to give the appearance of me having a big belly. Could I keep the loss from him until our court date? I would try to avoid him at all costs and I pray that when he does find out that we're not alone together. I didn't own any baggy or loose clothing because I had a cute shape and I liked to flaunt it with a wardrobe that had a flattering fit. Demetrius knew every curve of my body and if he was able to get close enough he would notice I wasn't pregnant anymore. The question is, would he think I had an abortion or that I lost the baby?

I became friendlier with a couple of the guards so I could get my hands on their work schedules. I made small talk whenever I came and went so they would become familiar with me. I wanted to gain their trust. I was being very sneaky, but a girl had to do what a girl had to do. I was trying to survive so I needed to distract them any way I could, even if this meant using my feminine charm.

I had appointments to look at a couple of potential apartments so I asked Mike to go with me. I loved his company. He would give me an honest opinion of the places. The first place we looked at was a dump and it wasn't move-in-ready. The carpet was nasty, the plumbing fixtures were old and outdated and the on-site manager told me not to expect new carpet or any updates.

I passed on that one and drove a few blocks away to the next apartment. The street was lined with trees which would provide lots of shade in the summertime and it was in a cul-de-sac. This was an open apartment that we could enter and walk around on our own. There were applications left on the kitchen counter for anyone who was interested. The place was advertised as a one-bedroom with a large walk-in closet. Clearly this was false advertisement because the closet wasn't large enough to enter and wouldn't hold a fraction of my clothes not to mention my shoes. Mike and I both chuckled at the thought of me trying to squeeze everything into that tiny closet.

We had one more apartment to look at. It was closer to downtown Los Angeles and was listed as a loft. I could live in a loft as long as it was spacious and was occupied by working tenants. We talked and laughed on the drive downtown. Mike told me about his newest lover who was a professor at City College. They met while he waited to have his car serviced. They had been dating for a few weeks and were having this hot and steamy romantic love affair. I was happy for him and hoped it worked out long term.

We were getting close to the address, but didn't see a lot of parking on the street. I had to have a parking space and didn't want to struggle with driving in circles every night after work. We turned around and found parking on the opposite side of the street. Once inside the building, I couldn't wait to see upstairs. I rang the buzzer for someone to show the loft. Mike and I were taken upstairs on an elevator to the available unit.

When the door was opened, I was pleasantly surprised at how large it was. There was floor to ceiling windows on three of the walls and large closets with built in shoe racks. I was impressed with the grey paint, matching new carpet and best of all this fit into my budget perfectly. I looked around and tried to visually see my furnishings there. I was sold. This was going be my new place, I could feel it. I asked if there were many people interested and when the earliest I could move in was. There was one other person who was interested, but didn't pass the credit check. I filled out an application, paid the credit check fee and expressed how much I would like to move in within the next two weeks. I had to wait three days to find out if I was accepted.

Mike must have been reading my mind all along. After we got out the elevator, he said "girl, you must throw a big party if you get this place."

"If I pull the move off, I will throw the biggest party ever Mike."

He thought it was gorgeous and so did I. Mike asked about me feeling safe if I moved there. I would definitely feel much safer than where I lived now. If I planned the move right, Demetrius and his inside man would never know my new location. I would need to take extra precaution when leaving work to avoid being followed. I shared my plan with Mike on how I was going to get the guards' work schedule. He thought it was clever, but warned me to be careful. I drove Mike home and headed back to my place to work on my plan.

I went home and wrote out a list of things I would need to do in order to make my move quick and easy. I would need to reserve a moving company, buy boxes and schedule a few vacation days off from work. My supervisor was very understanding and aware of what I was going through so the time wouldn't be an issue. The more I was away from the office, the less likely there was a chance of Demetrius and I having a confrontation there.

I was jumping the gun a little and didn't even know if I would get the place I found. I'm positive about most things and hoped for the phone to ring with good news. Until then, I would wait for the perfect time to go to the security station to make my move on the guard schedule. Demetrius had not shown himself in a while, but I knew he was watching. If it wasn't him directly, it was one of his men doing the dirty work for him.

I called to check in on Beverly before turning in. The phone rang several times before she picked up.

"Hello."

"Beverly, this is Arlene. Are you okay? I was worried sick about you. Have you calmed down after your visit from Demetrius?"

"Arlene, I'm glad you called. I thought you were upset with me." "I know you did what you had to do Beverly. You're my girl and I can't stay upset with you. Everything will be alright once this nightmare is over."

Too Scared to Run

I slept in the next morning, but I had to rise and shine in order to make my doctor appointment on time. While I was getting ready I remembered not to apply make-up so the doctor could look at my scar. The more I stared at my face in the mirror, the more I wanted to breakdown and cry. I hated what it looked like without foundation or powder. I always prided myself on taking care of my skin, my hair and body. The face looking back at me through the mirror wasn't me and I hated it.

There was no time for self-pity. It was so unlike me to have those types of feelings. I left for the doctor, waving and smiling at the guards in the station with them waving back; all except for Demetrius' guy. He stared as he usually did when I passed by. While he was on duty, I knew he wouldn't be following me so I smiled at the little freedom it gave me.

My face was healing right on schedule and I wouldn't need plastic surgery unless I chose to do it as an elective surgery. I would have to pay all costs out of pocket. I was made aware the procedure is costly if I elected to have it. My doctor prescribed a low dose of sleeping pill that would help me relax and get a good night's sleep. My money was going toward a bigger purchase so looking flawless wasn't high on my priority list. I had to move and get away from Demetrius. On my way to work, I saw a storage company and decided to pick up some boxes. I could start packing early so I wouldn't tire myself out trying to do it all at once like last time.

My supervisor came to my office and asked to speak with me. She told me Demetrius was at the office looking for me. She told him I wasn't in yet, but he didn't seem convinced. He pushed past her and headed for my office to look for himself. Before leaving, he knocked over the computer from my desk and told her he would be back. . I was embarrassed at his actions, I apologized for his stupidity and thought of what he might do if he did come back. She picked up the computer and sat it back on my desk. I knew from the look on her face that she was afraid for me and the other staff. Seeing first-hand what he was capable of would make any normal person fear facing him again. She suggested that I go to the police because she couldn't afford to put anyone in jeopardy of getting hurt. I understood and left immediately.

When I arrived at the police station, I filed a report explaining what my supervisor described as a violent act. He destroyed private property and acted in a threatening manner promising to return to see me. The officer told me because I wasn't an eye witness that I couldn't submit the report; my supervisor would need to come down and file a report on Demetrius. I pleaded with the officer to take my report and explained that I was afraid for my life. Demetrius already attacked me, made me lose my baby and permanently scarred my face. He looked at me holding the paper out in front of me. With a little compassion he took it out of my hand and said he would give it to the detective who was over the ongoing case.

I couldn't go back to work, I was too scared to go home. I panicked and didn't know what to do. I stopped at a park so I could think. I called the manager at the loft

"Hello, this is Arlene Simmons. I'm calling to ask if my credit check went through."

"Miss Simmons, I was looking for your application to give you a call. Your credit check did go through. If you're still interested in the Loft, you can move in. You will need to bring in a deposit before picking up the keys."

I threw my hands up, looked towards the heavens and said, "thank you Jesus for being here for me right on time."

Rossilyn Lillard

I'll come by with my deposit tomorrow. Thank you."

Chapter 26

Now that I had found a place to move, I had to get a look at that guard schedule. Once I found out what days and times Demetrius' stalking ass homeboy worked, I could reserve the moving company so they could load up my shit and get me out of there before I was found out. I came up with an idea that might work. Men couldn't resist a good-looking woman, especially if she had on tight jeans or showed a little cleavage. If she had a big ass, she could have the world.

I took a chance and went home. I changed out of my work suit and pulled on a pair of the tightest jeans I could find, a skimpy tank top and a pair of boots completed my ensemble. I walked to the security station and asked one of the guys if they knew where I could get a good price on some tires for my car. I told them about the flat I caught the other day and that I didn't want to take any chances of that happening again. Just as I was hoping, both guards on duty came over to me. I leaned over the open window showing some cleavage and their eyes went straight to my chest. They were drooling as if they had never seen breast before.

As sexy as I could, I asked I could come inside and keep them company. One of them came to attention and said it was against policy to allow anyone inside the booth. "Oh, come on," I said. "I won't tell anybody if you don't tell." The second guard said that it would be alright for a few minutes. He opened the door and pointed to a chair in the corner. I sat on top of one of the desks instead swinging my legs back and forth. They introduced themselves to me and I told them my name. While we talked, I looked around the desk for the clipboard with the schedule attached, but it wasn't on the desk. I slid off the desk deliberately knocking some papers to the floor with my hand. The first guard immediately took action and bent to pick up the papers while I scoured the small room for the schedule. I spotted it on the back of the door but it was too far away for me to read it. I thanked the guys for the visit and headed out the door. I stopped with my hand on the doorknob just long enough to search the list. I found what I came for and left. I could feel both pairs of eyes staring as I twisted away.

Mr. Inside Man was off on Thursdays and Sundays so I reserved the moving company for the following Thursday between seven o'clock am and noon. I preferred the weekday to move instead of Sunday because no one would expect it. Demetrius could be lurking around on the weekends even if his friend wasn't working. I needed to pack and call to transfer the utilities to my new address. Living near downtown would be a different experience than living in the inner city. It meant more traffic and busyness, but I wouldn't have to worry about noise from children playing outside. The loft was an adult's only building centered between two commercial properties.

 Before relaxing for the day, I closed my windows, double locked the front door and settled on the breeze from the balcony. I was on the second floor so there was no way up except by using the stairs. I wasn't comfortable in my own home now that Demetrius knew where I was. I couldn't think of what may have provoked him to go to my job. He never went there before, even though he knew where I worked. When I left for work in the mornings, he would leave for work. At least I thought he was going to work. He was out there doing his street thing as "D." Slinging drugs and bringing the devil's money home to pay rent and bills. I couldn't fathom the idea of him being on a street corner or riding up and down the street in pimped out cars dressed in gang attire. This was beyond me being able to wrap my head around. We lived together and I never saw one item of gang attire. Where was he keeping his gear? Where did he keep his drugs and weapons because they sure were not in my apartment?

Everything about Demetrius was a lie. I thought I was a good judge of character, but not when it came to the men I fell in love with. I didn't use my brain, I used my heart. I fell hard for men who were charming, attentive and nicely dressed. Demetrius was all of those things. When I thought of him and his family, I just don't see any resemblance. Their criminal activities, rap sheets and the control they had over the streets was in unison. Demetrius was the better looking of all his brothers. Hell, he even looked better than his sister. Maybe they had different fathers or something because the ugly gene skipped him.

I laid on the couch and watched old western movies. Westerns were my grandmother's favorites. I felt her near whenever I watched them. A good shoot-em up always helped me relax. I remembered the sleeping pills my doctor prescribed and took one with a glass of water. By the time it took effect it would be time for and I could rest easy. I forgot to bring in the packing boxes upstairs so I would have to start packing tomorrow.

Too Scared to Run

I was still on the couch when the morning light woke me up. . At least I knew the sleeping pills worked. I slept straight through the night. I had things to do and couldn't afford to prance around. I changed into some lounge clothes and went to the car to get the boxes. The parking garage was empty and quiet. I didn't like going down there alone. As I was taking the stack of boxes out of the trunk, the security car rolled up. The driver was none other than Mr. Inside Man himself. He slowly drove my way and asked, "Are you moving Miss Lady?" "No, just packing up clothes for the Good Will." I responded. He continued past making his rounds through the complex.

With the boxes tucked under my arm, I took the elevator back to my unit. That was a close call. I hope I sounded convincing enough so Mr. Inside Man wouldn't mention the boxes to Demetrius. I started with the kitchen, packing anything I wouldn't be needed in the next two weeks. Pots, pans, glassware and canned goods all fit nicely into the boxes. I subscribed to the daily paper and had plenty to wrap the glassware. I left out enough to get by with for the next week or so. Next, I packed away any clothes in drawers and hall cabinets, being careful not to crowd the boxes so my sweaters wouldn't wrinkle.

Rossilyn Lillard

My bedroom closet was saved for moving day. Those clothes would be carried out on hangers. My shoes would be packed last.

I reserved a large truck so everything could be moved in one trip. When I pull out the complex next Thursday, I wanted it to be for the last time. When Mr. Inside Man, returned on his next shift, my keys would already be turned in and I would be gone. My security deposit would be sent to my job, that way I wouldn't be leaving a trail that could lead Demetrius to my new place. He had me followed before, but this time I was better prepared to cover my tracks. Demetrius and his gang didn't venture downtown because it landed them into rival gang territory. There could be bloodshed if a gang member crossed their boundaries. Anybody caught slipping with the wrong color on might not make it back alive.

Since we had other offices, I put in for a transfer to a place closer to my house. To really switch things up a bit, I requested a different shift as well. Moving wouldn't be enough to keep Demetrius, everything about me would need to change if I truly intended to throw him off my trail. I would need to keep him guessing where I was and what I was doing at all times. I hated giving up my condo, but I couldn't stay anyplace I didn't feel safe or peaceful.

The ringing of the phone shook me because I didn't recall giving my new number out for one and for two no one knew I was home. Hesitantly, I answered. Demetrius was on the other end. He told me he called my job and was told that I didn't show up for work. He claimed to be calling to see if everything was alright. He sked if I was home because of morning sickness due to the pregnancy. I hesitated to answer him because, I didn't want to lie, but at the same time I didn't want to give him a reason to blow up. I turned the conversation to him and asked how his family was doing. He told me his mother was still trying to get over the death of his brother.

I must not be thinking clearly because if I were, I would have known Demetrius could easily get my new number. I had to give it to management office so security could call and announce visitors. Mr. Inside Man was on his job and didn't miss anything. He was trying to feel me out. His inside man probably mentioned seeing me with boxes and with a number change he figured something was up. I knew I needed to keep my eyes open and be careful over the next few days. I couldn't afford for Demetrius to find out my plans to move.

I needed to get another look at the loft so I drove down and took my time to walk around. I wanted to strategically place my furnishings in a way that would give me the best view. It was spacious, but didn't have any dividers so I would need to use beads or partitions to separate the bedroom area from the living room space. Before leaving, I took note of a few extra things I would need to buy to make it my own. I would have Mike come over to add the finishing touches after everything was unpacked.

Not being able to go to church and praise with the other saints was wearing on me. I drove to the church to talk with the pastor and found him hosing down the parking lot. When he saw me he turned off the water and greeted me with a big hug and smile.

"You've been on my mind a lot lately, Arlene. How have you been?"

"I've been alright. I miss attending Sunday services." I sighed. This isn't the best thing for me right now."

"I tried calling you, but your number was disconnected."

"I changed my number and I apologize for not calling you."

I wrote down my new number for him and followed him into the church where we sat and talked.

"Please pray that God give me strength and courage to testify against Demetrius."

"You're doing the right thing." He said a prayer for me and I left.

I felt more alive than I had in a long time. My spirit was uplifted after visiting with my pastor. He was a good man, a father figure who was always there to give me guidance and steer me in the right direction. He was a forgiving man and lived his life in a manner pleasing to God. He encouraged me to stay in the word, remain faithful and never give up. . If I did that he guaranteed God would protect me and I would come out in victory. Even though I made mistakes and put myself in some sticky situations, God always saw me through.

Demetrius never mentioned going to see Beverly or going to my job. He liked playing the crazy game and I played it right along with him. I didn't ask about either. I checked in with my supervisor to see if Demetrius ever came back but he hadn't. I was feeling light-headed from not eating breakfast before I got out for the day. I stopped at a small café in my old neighborhood to have lunch. I headed to a booth in the back when I saw

Demetrius' sister sitting at a table by herself. I walked over to say hi and she invited me to join her. I hadn't seen her since the funeral. I ordered a sandwich and soup, she ordered a bowl of chili. She asked if I was excited about having a baby. I told her that I never thought I would have children and I was still getting used to the idea.

She was quiet for a while and then asked if I had forgiven Demetrius for hitting me. I had not forgiven Demetrius and didn't know if I ever could. She should understand once she found out he killed our baby. She went on about Demetrius never being in love with a woman the way he loved me. She also told me he was jealous and possessive. Well, this was certainly true, but I found out the hard way. Why was everyone telling me now what they should have told me in the beginning? If I had known the truth I would never have taken a second look at him. I would still be happy and the terrible chain of events would have never happened. I wouldn't have suffered the loss of my unborn child. I never seen its little face, but I loved it all the same.

It was getting close to moving day and the butterflies were in full force in my stomach. I was all packed and ready for the movers. I had sheets draped over my furniture to avoid dirt getting on anything. I cleaned for the next couple of days, wiping down the cabinets, cleaning the stove and refrigerator. I saved the bathroom for last so I could clean the tub and shower for the last time. Everything would be spotless so there would be no reason for me not to get every dime of my deposit back.

Chapter 27

I was up early with excitement, filled joy. I was getting away from Demetrius for a second time. The movers would be arriving at any minute. I took all my important papers and put them in the car along with a few decorative items and mirrors from the walls. I didn't want to risk them getting misplaced or broken. I sat on a stack of boxes as I waited for the movers but grew impatient. I called the moving company.

"Good morning. I have a reservation today. What time will the movers arrive?

"May I have your last name Miss?"

"My last name is Simmons."

"Your reservation was cancelled."

"Cancelled? Would you double-check please? I didn't cancel the reservation."

"Miss your reservation was cancelled. He repeated my name and address, where I was moving from and the new address. All the information was correct.

When I heard a knock on the door, I figured the guy on the phone didn't know what he was talking about. It had to be the movers. I didn't even check the peek-hole, I just swung open the door. There stood Demetrius and Calvin dressed in street clothes with rags hanging out of their pockets and everything. Demetrius pushed me back inside as they both walked in. He asked me why I thought I could move without saying anything to him. He said he knew what I did at all times and knew about me calling the moving company. He made me feel so stupid for not expecting something to go wrong with this move.

Calvin Edwards was usually silent, but he stepped up and did a little talking today. He told me, "Miss Lady, I've been following you since you moved from your old place." He told me that after I had Demetrius arrested is when he started. He followed me every day as I left to and from work and any other places I went. He even had my phone tapped and knew all about my conversations. He kept Demetrius abreast of everything about me. Demetrius never took his eyes off of me. He remained quiet as his main man talked to me. . I looked toward the couch where I hid my gun behind the pillows and he noticed. He reached behind his back and pulled my gun out of his waistband and asked, "is this what you are looking for?"

At that point, I was feeling hopeless and didn't know how I would get away from them. Demetrius stepped closer to where I was standing. He had just one questions for me, what happened to the baby? He told me he knew I was no longer pregnant and wanted to know what happened. He told me I had nothing to be afraid of and urged me to tell the truth. I looked back and forth between Demetrius and Calvin, but I couldn't form any words. "You killed it when you attacked me that day at my old apartment. I yelled! I needed surgery to patch up my face and the trauma caused me to hemorrhage. The baby didn't survive."

Out of respect Calvin, with his head slightly bowed opened the door. He left me and Demetrius alone. Demetrius pulled me close to him and held me tight. I stiffened to feel his body so close to mine. The man who hurt me, the man who killed our baby was standing close enough for me to feel his breath. Blood rushed to my head and my heart started pounding. Was I happy to be back in his arms or was fear gripping me? Whichever the feeling was, I didn't like it. I tried to push back but his hold on me was too strong.

There were no words spoken as we stood in the middle of a room filled with boxes. I would never be able to move now. I was being stalked like an animal after prey. Demetrius finally released his hold on me and allowed me to breathe. He told me he was sorry and would make it up to me. He went on about us still being young and could always have more babies. He told me we could start over and build a life together. He told me that he was ready to marry me and make me his wife.

I fainted as his words reached my ears. Was I really hearing him say us? There was no more us. He killed that dream when he violently struck me. I pressed charges on him for a reason. Purposely wanting him to go to jail for his actions. The trial was in less than a month and I still planned on following-through with my testimony against him. The district attorney was trying to nail Demetrius for years and if I could help him lock this maniac up, then I would.

When I came to my full senses, I was laying on my bed. My shoes were off and a blanket was draped over my legs. I didn't see Demetrius and hoped he was already gone. I didn't know whether to lay there and pretend it was all a dream or get up. How long had I been out? I was startled at what I saw when I came out of my bedroom. Boxes were unpacked and my things had all been put back where they belonged. The sheets were gone from the furniture, the pictures were back on the walls. Even the pots, pans and dishes were put back into the kitchen cabinets. I went back into my bedroom to look in the closet, not only were my clothes there but, Demetrius' belongings were too. How did he have time to do all of this? I couldn't have been out for more than a few minutes at the most.

I stepped further into the living room and there was Demetrius sitting on the balcony. I went to him and asked "what are you doing and why did you unpack my things?"

"You're not going anywhere, Arlene. I unpacked the boxes while you were sleeping."

"I refuse to live here with you, Demetrius. Pease, let me go."

"We're a couple. Accept it. You belong to me and no other man will ever have you."

He forced me call the DA to tell him I changed my mind and wouldn't be testifying in court. Making the call to the DA was difficult because he was counting on me. I was being forced against my will to do something I didn't want to do. If I didn't testify, Demetrius would be free and the charges against him would be thrown out. That's exactly how Demetrius went free of prosecutions on other case. He used intimidation tactics to scare off witnesses. He would threaten to hurt them and their families, he would have them followed until they were too afraid to pursue sending him to jail. I listened to every word he said. It took all of my strength not to cry out. I couldn't show any weakness to him, so I followed his instructions and made the call.

I made the call and was put through to the district attorney. I told him Demetrius and I were back together and it was all a misunderstanding. I told him not to expect me in court because I was no longer testifying. He asked if everything was alright and wanted to know why the sudden change of heart. I told him I had time to think about what happened and didn't feel it necessary to pursue charges any longer. He asked if everything was alright one final time. I thanked him and hung up.

I would die before I allowed this man to control me and keep me as if I was property. I've prayed too hard for God to deliver me from this situation and keep me safe. I was depending on His will to do what He said He would do. This good girl could go bad, if that's what it took to get away from this monster. Demetrius was unbothered by what he had me do. He sat there as if we had never been apart. Ice had to run through his veins for him to be so cruel and callous.

I went back into my bedroom so I could think. I needed to get away. Not only did I have Demetrius to contend with, but I had his right hand man looking over my shoulder. If

Rossilyn Lillard

Demetrius was so tough why didn't he do his own dirty work? I would have a better chance getting away from Calvin than Demetrius. For Demetrius, this was personal. He was taking ownership of what he believed to be his. He wouldn't let me out of his sight for too long in fear of me trying to escape.

Looking through my bedroom window, the drop wasn't that far. If I could jump or climb down, I could run to my car and drive off. I looked for my keys, but did not see them anywhere. My purse was on the night stand, but my keys were not inside. I must have left them on the kitchen counter while waiting for the movers. I was sweaty and nervous and overthinking my entire situation. I had to calm down and think rationally. I did the only thing I know. I prayed. I dropped to my knees, closed my eyes and prayed to my Lord and Savior to lead me to freedom. I asked Him to remove all the obstacles in my way. Right now, my only obstacle was Demetrius.

Demetrius was standing in the doorway as I opened my eyes rising from the floor. He was holding a tray of food and asked if I was hungry. I took the tray and took a few bites from the sandwich he made for me. All the while I was thinking about my next move. Would he allow me to come and go as I pleased or would I be held captive and at his beck and call? What about my job, my friends? What would they say or think about me? My friends Beverly and Mike, would they ever see me again?

Demetrius sat on the bed beside me and asked how I was feeling. I told him I was feeling alright, but confused about what he was doing. He told me from the first day we met, he knew that I was the one woman to his life complete. I was the one he wanted as his life partner and mother of his children. He added the only reason that he struck out at me was because he was hurt that I would even think about putting him out of my life. There was talk around the neighborhood about the damage he did to my face and he was ashamed his hand was the weapon. He was starting to scare me when he told me he couldn't live without me.

Lame excuses couldn't be accepted from a man who was known to be dangerous and uncivilized. There were enough gangs out on the streets for him to fight and shoot. He didn't have to put his hands on me. If you want to keep a woman by your side the thing to do is to show her that you want her in your life. Do the things it took to keep her and show her you love her. If a man does that, his woman would always be by his side.

Rossilyn Lillard

Violence causes bitterness and hatred, even in a Christian such as myself. I'm bitter and now that he has forced his way back into my life against my will, hatred was not far behind.

He was so right at the beginning and I was living the fairytale every woman or girl dreamt of. His double life has since been exposed and I know I can't love a man of his caliber. He could force me to be with him, but he couldn't make me love him. The longer he keeps me here, the bitterer I will become and he will soon find out I'm not as weak as I appear. He will find out I too have been keeping a little secret and my skeletons will begin creeping out of my closet. Demetrius better keep both eyes open.

I tried avoiding Demetrius, but it wasn't easy in my small condo. He followed me around like I was going to disappear or something. I didn't want to look at him, didn't want to talk to him. I did not want him here. I did not know he dressed was in a t-shirt, khakis and croaker sack shoes. It was as if the clothes changed his demeanor. The way he walked had a gangster lean to it and he wore a snarl on his face. I overheard him talking to Calvin. He told him to leave and said he would call him if he needed him. He was a stranger that I had never met before.

What did he do with Demetrius, my Mr. Right?

"What started your double life," I asked. He turned to look at me and for an instant, he was the Demetrius I knew. He told me this is the way it is when you come from a family involved in gangs, violence and drugs. I understood his reasoning, but I also believed that he made a conscious choice to keep the tradition alive. He told me his parents were opposites, father a minister spending most of his time in church. His mother rarely went to church, she stayed at home, did a lot of drinking, running around in the streets jumping from bar to bar. He said his father loved her, but got fed up and left.

After his father split, his mother lost control of his older brothers. They did want they wanted and ended up hanging out in the streets joining gangs. After joining gangs, they got involved with prostituting women to pay for their drugs. Demetrius was more like his father and enjoyed going to church and reading the bible. He told me, when he was growing up he would mimic his father preaching in the pulpit. He would stand on a stack of phone books with his brothers as the congregation and he would preach.

Demetrius told me that he was torn between his love for God and the streets. He was pressured by his brothers and friends to put the bible down and act like a real man. They told him a real man had a hustle out in the streets and took what they wanted from others. He took the only way he could to stay alive and was jumped in the gang at the age of sixteen. He never liked what he did, but had no choice. It was either that or lose his life. Demetrius hid his religion from his brothers and street family, in fear they would kick him out of the gang. He told me God knew his heart and would forgive him of his sins.

Demetrius asked for my forgiveness for lying to me about who he really was. He told me he was still the same person and that he loved me. I told him I could forgive him for hurting me, but could not forget that he took an innocent life. An unborn child needed the safety of its mother's womb for nine months. Our baby didn't have a chance at survival because its lifeline was stripped away.

He reached out to console me, but I backed away. He left me alone. The phone rang and before I could get to it Demetrius answered. I didn't know what the other person was saying, but I could tell who it was from how he responded. It was the manager from the loft I was supposed to move into. Demetrius told them I needed my deposit back and something came up so I wouldn't be moving in. He told them he would be sending someone over in the morning to pick up the check.

Demetrius was serious about me staying with him. He told me not to worry about my job because he would take care of me. According to him, I needed to stay home and take care of his needs and the condo. He was already looking for a larger place for us to move into because he wanted a backyard for our children to play in. I had no intention of him fathering any child of mine. Especially since I knew the whole truth about who is really was. Heaven forbid I have a son. I wouldn't place such a burden on a child that I birthed into this world.

I needed a way to contact the District Attorney. On that last phone call I was counting on him knowing that something must be wrong. In the past, I was too adamant about going to court. To throw away all the work we did to build the case at the last minute was be stupid on my part. This was not the movies where SWAT would come crashing through the door taking down the assailant and rescuing the innocent victim. I had to find my own way out.

After begging all week, Demetrius finally gave in and allowed me to go to church. Not alone though. He came with me. I prepared myself ahead of time for the stares and shameful looks I would get from the congregation. They knew of my history with Demetrius and were surprised as we walked into church together. We found a seat near the middle and waited for service to begin. The ushers passed out hand fans and collection envelopes but Demetrius nodded that we didn't need one. I took one and told him I still needed to pay my tithes to the church.

Service went on as usual with a few members turning and whispering about me being in church with the man that scarred my face. Christians were too fake. Gossiping in the church and passing judgement is what they were all taught not to do. That didn't stop the few who didn't know how to mind their own business. Other than that, service was good. When it was time for the sermon, pastor stood and asked us to stand in prayer. Before bowing his head his eyes locked with mine. His look was of disbelief, mine was that of despair. I wanted to run, but my feet would not move.

At the end of the sermon the ushers came around with the collection plate passing it down each aisle. Demetrius got up to go to the restroom and this was my opportunity to

Too Scared to Run

reach out for help. I took a pen out of my purse to write out a check, on the back I wrote, help, please call the police. I sealed it in the envelope and dropped it into the plate as Demetrius came back to sit down. The collection plate passed in front of him, but he did not drop anything in it.

The church doors were open for anyone who wanted to give their life to Jesus. The Deacons stood at the front of the church with outstretched arms to draw someone to the altar. While the ushers were finishing collecting the offering, I didn't take my eyes off that collection plate; until I saw them walk to the back where they would count the money. One women joined church accepting Jesus as her personal Savior. That was always a joy for me to witness. Demetrius sat there unmoved. Church was over and it was time to leave. A few members came up to us to say a few words, but most ignored us. I looked for pastor but did not see him in the crowd of people. We headed out the door and I was relieved to see police surrounding the church.

I said, "thank you, Jesus" as they rushed toward Demetrius. He wasn't expecting it. As two of the Officers grabbed his hands back to place the cuffs on his wrist, he twisted and jerked trying to get away. They wrestled him to the ground while he looked at me as if I betrayed him. The first Officer recognized Demetrius from previous street encounters. "D Weaver", he said as he patted him down finding my gun tucked into his waistband. "You are being charged with felony kidnapping, possession of a loaded firearm and other miscellaneous charges." He was read his Miranda Rights and put into the back of the patrol car. Another Officer came over and took the report from me. I let him know I would be in contact with the District Attorney regarding my testimony against Demetrius.

I watched as the patrol car drove Demetrius away. Many of the church members were still in the parking lot and couldn't believe what they witnessed. Pastor walked over to me and put this arm around my shoulder. I was comforted by this presence. One of the Deacons saw what I wrote on the check and he took it to the Pastor. He wasted no time calling the police when he saw it was my name on the front of that check. He knew something was out of place with me sitting beside Demetrius. I took a chance and it worked out in my favor. My God was always right on time.

I couldn't celebrate so soon. I still had to go home and chances are Calvin Edwards would be somewhere near. I needed to act before Demetrius was able to make his first phone call. I called Beverly and Mike to let them know what happened and told them I would be out of touch for a while. They both offered to help me but this was bigger than any of us could handle. I needed to go to the Big Dog to get rid of my problem. I was going to collect on a huge debt owed to me from someone in my past. It would not end up pretty.

I packed a few suitcases as fast as I could, hating to leave my personal belongings behind. I couldn't wait a minute longer if I wanted to escape this nightmare I was in. Once I got settled, I would call and ask the property management to pack up my apartment and place everything in storage.

On my way out the door, my phone rang. Mike calling to tell me word was going around that Demetrius escaped. He was being transferred to Men's Central Jail downtown with other inmates, but got away when they took him out of a patrol car to put him in a van. He told me it was all over the news. I rushed out and headed downstairs to my car. I just started driving to put as much distance between me and Demetrius as I could.

The detective on the case promised me were going to search high and low until they found Demetrius so he could stand trial for what he did to me. Now he had an escape to add to his record. I was a little skeptical and feel that he was clever enough to evade the police and taunt me forever. Demetrius was a very dangerous man and would do anything to take what he believed to be his. Each time the police were close to him, someone, would tip them off and he would run before they arrived. His luck has to run out eventually.

I wanted to be there face-to-face with him. I wanted to spit in his face to let him know how little of a human he was before they shoot and kill him. I want to look him in the eyes while shouting "shoot him, kill him!" Those were thoughts of anger and fear. I could never wish death upon him despite what he put me through.

Now, if they drove him to a dark alley, on the way to the police station and commence to giving him a good old fashioned ass whooping, I could live with that. It would give me a sense of satisfaction. That brought a smile to my face but the struggle was real and I didn't know who I was anymore. I loved God and I trusted Him, but the evil voices in my head were talking louder and louder. They were cheering me on when thoughts of revenge and murder crept in. I had to think like Demetrius if I wanted my life back. I had to rethink my plan in getting to safety because waiting on the law might bring my terrifying adventure to an end.

I waited for news that Demetrius was caught, but nothing was mentioned on the news. It was two long years of moving, running and fighting and I was exhausted. I just couldn't run anymore. I prayed night and day that I would come out of this alive. It's been weeks since I've heard anything from the detective or the District Attorney. What was happening? Why hadn't they taken him into custody yet? How could Demetrius be out there in the streets and not be seen by the police? He was eluding the police at every turn and hiding with the help of friends and family. It must have been frustrating for them too. Something has to happen, I was drained. With little sleep and no appetite, the stress was beginning to show outwardly. My hair was falling out, I had bags under my eyes and I've lost weight. I needed rest, I needed rest soon.

Chapter 28

I stopped at a motel on the west side. I was too damn tired to drive any more. I didn't take my luggage out the car, I just checked-in. I locked the door and put the chain on. I didn't see anyone following me, but needed the extra security. It wasn't too long before I feel off to sleep. I wanted to catch a few hours and then hit the road again. I had a long drive ahead of me so I needed to be rested and alert. I only paid for four hours so I had to make the best use of the time. The small, outdated television took a while to warm up before the screen came on. I was hoping for an update on Demetrius, but his capture wasn't mentioned.

I threw some water on my face before leaving and headed out to my car. I looked around where I thought I parked but my car was gone. This cannot be happening to me not with Demetrius on my tail. I went to the motel office to ask if they saw anybody close to my car. I used their phone to call the police to report my car stolen. I walked around waiting for the police when I spotted Demetrius' right hand man. He was leaning against my car, across the street. He was looking in the opposite direction and didn't see me. I started walking back to the motel office when I heard him call my name.

Too Scared to Run

I ran as fast as I could, but before I could reach the office, Demetrius came around the corner of the motel and stopped me. He grabbed me by the arm and led me across the street. He shoved me into the passenger seat of my own car with Calvin trailing in his car. He slapped me across the mouth with a backhand, jerking my head to the side. "You will never get away from me, Arlene, so stop trying." I couldn't defend myself against him. He knew when I breathed and always had eyes watching.

Demetrius pulled over on the side of the street. He got out the car, came over to the passenger door, opened it and pulled me out of the car. He jerked my face towards his to get my full attention, He put his hands around my throat. His grip became tighter as I twisted and jerked to get away from him. I tried to yell, but had no voice due to his hold on me. I saw darkness all around me, but tried to hold on to life as I sank to the pavement.

I felt hands around my waist and my legs as I was violently tossed into the backseat of the car. I screamed as loud l as I could. At least I thought I was screaming. With the windows rolled up, no one could hear me, no one could hear my cries for help. I don't know how long we drove and I didn't care. I just wanted to wake up from one of the worst nightmares of my life. Demetrius started yelling at me and beating the steering wheel with his hands. "Why do you keep running away from me, Arlene, why? I made one mistake and you won't forgive me! Then you set me up at a church of all places!" He told me he would die for me if he had to and that running from the police would be easy.

I wept as quietly as I could in the backseat without Demetrius ever giving notice. "Why won't you just let me go? Why do you keep coming after me? I don't want you, I don't love you," He ignored my cries. I didn't have anything to lose so I kicked at the back window as hard as I could but it wouldn't break. I tried hard to break it or to get someone's attention for help. The car started swerving as he grabbed my legs so I would stop the kicking. He reached back and gave me a backhand with all his might. he knocked me out and when I returned to consciousness, we were in the hood. Demetrius had his Right Hand Man go in the store to get an ice pack and a towel for my nose. His backhand broke my nose and blood was still running down the front of my face.

I rode with the towel and ice on my face. The painful throbbing was unbearable. I could barely breathe through my nostrils. I told Demetrius I needed to go to the emergency room. He snapped back telling me we were not going to the emergency room. He told me he would take care of me and nurse me back to health. It was only an hour ride from the motel Demetrius found me at, but time stood still. I was ready to get out of the car. I was getting nauseous and my throat felt as if it was closing.

He drove until we were back on the east side. He drove through the gate of my condo using my keycard. What the hell was he doing? I told property management that I had to leave and to put my things in storage. Why was he bringing me back here? He parked under the garage in my old space and then walked me to the elevator. I resisted, but he nudged me inside. We got out on the second floor where my condo was, he turned the key and pushed me inside.